Acknowledgements
A special word of thanks to AuthorHouse for
their support in publishing this book and for
all those who assisted me in this endeavor.
I am truly grateful for your support.

My Cosmic Quest
A SEARCH FOR ENLIGHTENMENT

Paul Gavan

authorHOUSE®

AuthorHouse™
1663 Liberty Drive
Bloomington, IN 47403
www.authorhouse.com
Phone: 1 (800) 839-8640

Published by AuthorHouse 05/06/2016

ISBN: 978-1-5246-0803-3 (sc)
ISBN: 978-1-5246-0802-6 (e)

Print information available on the last page.

Contents

Dedication
To all Light workers. May we stand strong in the light of
the Eternal Flame, burning forever
within the hearts of all beings.

You have come here to learn to love and be happy in the constructs and confines of the force fields of this planet Earth and, at the same time, to assist others around you in this achievement. You are experiencing this moment as part of a familiar time frame, and yet the evolutionary leap has already taken place. All there is to do is to be. In being, there is a great joy and a powerful creative potential.

—The Family of Light

Preface

I learned from my spirit guides — the Family of Light, that humanity is in this world but not of it. Speaking to me through a medium, the Family of Light described a veil of illusion that catches even those of us who know, prompting us to forget that there is a connection between ourselves and the Divine and that, as human beings, we have the exalted charge to live in an awareness of that connection. My spirit guides told me that one of my main challenges is to remember my soul's higher purpose while living a life involved in the world. It is, I might add, certainly an involved life, and at times, I have found myself side-tracked.

I've known, for instance, from the very beginning, from the very first session back in November 1992, in which I was given information and instructions by my celestial guides, that I was supposed share their messages with others. And yet how often was it feasible — or appropriate or even welcome — for me to bring up my relationship with spirit guides in day-to-day conversations! Still, the Family of Light told me that communicating their messages would strengthen the connection between us, and so I began to consciously look for opportunities to do so.

Then, after several years, it occurred to me that I could write about my experiences, circulating these messages in a book. My Cosmic Quest is a result of that inspiration.

IN RETROSPECT I can see that this book is the most practical way for me to fulfill my perceived responsibility. The written word is extremely portable; a book can travel across space and time. A book about the Light, published in any place and at any time, has the potential of supporting the efforts of others who share their own experiences of the Light. And as all our efforts coalesce, together they will help to bring about the global shift in consciousness predicted in these pages by the Family of Light, a transformation whereby all of humanity will have the opportunity to heal itself and spiritually evolve.

May it be so!

PG

Belfast, N. Ireland

Chapter 1

From Belfast to Boston

One of my earliest memories is of the British Army arriving in Belfast, Northern Ireland. It was August 1969, and I was three years old. I was playing with my older sisters and some other children outside Greenways Store, the local grocery, when the soldiers pulled up in an armored vehicle. The soldiers stopped, went into the store, and came out tossing heaps of candy into the air. All of us laughed and scrambled to get our share. That day we went home happy; it seemed as if the British Army was there to take care of us. Another day the soldiers drove up our street in their armored vehicles and women came out of their houses with cups of tea for our new friends. While the soldiers took tea the children played with the equipment and weaponry inside the tanks. I was one of the lucky ones who got to look through the telescopic lens of an SLR rifle. Of course, the soldiers had covered the triggers of their guns, just to be safe.

This time came to be regarded as the "Honeymoon Period." Northern Ireland had been experiencing severe civil unrest, and the British government had sent military forces to help keep the peace. The British Army was there to prevent rival Irish factions from killing each other and sparking a full civil war. Honeymoons are generally last for a short period of time, and this view of the British Army as Ireland's benefactor was no exception.

What followed was the "Troubles," as Northern Ireland's recent embattled history has come to be known. Much has been written about the Troubles, a conflict that affected the lives of countless people – and still does. As a child of the Troubles, I became used to bombs and gunfire on the streets. Mayhem and strife was happening all around me, and although it wasn't constant, I witnessed it, so it seemed to me that it was just a part of life. I thought I was leading a normal life.

And in many ways I was. In West Belfast I grew up going to school, hanging out with my friends, playing football, listening to rock music, thinking about girls — doing all the things that teenagers do. On the other hand, few fourteen-year-olds go through a day like the one I experienced on May 12, 1981.

On that sunny spring day, I was once again standing with friends outside Greenways. Then a newsflash came up on the store's radio: the Irish Republican Francis Hughes had died after fifty-nine days on hunger strike. He was the second of ten Irish Republican prisoners to lose their lives attempting to be recognized as prisoners of war rather than criminals. The first of the Republican hunger strikers to die was Bobby Sands. I had watched Bobby Sands's funeral pass the

Suffolk estate where I lived; according to the BBC, more than seventy thousand people witnessed the procession.

Before we knew it, a crowd had gathered on the Stewartstown Road in front of Greenways, and the protesters, as was the custom in Northern Ireland, started banging their metal garbage bin lids on the road to broadcast their defiance. Then a British Saracen tank came into view heading straight for the crowd gathered in the middle of the road. From where I was standing, I could see it all.

People began running in all directions, some screaming and yelling, while others threw stones at the armored vehicle. The soldiers fired twice as they sped their Saracen past the crowd and towards a nearby police station. The plastic bullets went in two directions; I watched one shoot down Suffolk Avenue, a nearby street leading to my house, and the other go in the opposite direction into a field across the road from the Greenways store. When the tank had gone I ran down Suffolk Avenue and discovered a friend had recovered one of the bullets. "I got it! I got it!" he yelled triumphantly. "So you did, Mick! Let me hold it mate," I pleaded. Mick allowed me to examine it briefly.

It would eventually be acknowledged that these plastic bullets, just like the one Mick showed me, made of PVC, three-and-a-half inches long, and one-and–a-half inches in diameter, would be responsible for the deaths of fourteen people, including nine children. Unfortunately, one of those children was also at Greenways on this fateful day. Just as I gave Mick back his souvenir plastic bullet we heard the cry of the crowd. "Someone was hit! Someone was hit!"

"Where?" we yelled.

"Over in the field!"

We all ran over across the road to the field opposite Greenways. I saw a small cluster of people had gathered close to a hedge. I couldn't see through them but I could hear someone say that a young girl had been hit, and that an ambulance was on its way.

As I turned and headed back to find my friends I didn't know then how serious her injury was, or where she was struck, but I learned later that the plastic bullet had proved fatal and she had died the following day. People said she had been to Greenways on a shopping errand for her mother. I knew at some point she must have walked right by me as I hung outside the store. Her name was Julie Livingstone and she was only fourteen years old – the same age as me.

Years later I would often return to that very spot where this killing occurred and where a small memorial was eventually built in Julie's honor.

It wasn't until I was twenty-one that I started wondering why people — men, women, and young people like Julie — were being killed all over Northern Ireland, with no end to the violence in sight. It was now July 1987 and I had recently moved from my parent's house in West Belfast to the university area of the city to share an apartment. There were a lot of young people living in the area with different religious and political backgrounds, yet relative harmony existed amongst the mostly-student population.

One night, standing at the back during Mass in the Queen's University Chaplaincy, I felt an urge to turn to the spirit of Jesus for answers to the troubles of Northern Ireland. I'd never thought of myself as a religious person, and I usually found Mass to be quite boring, but I liked the chaplaincy priest as he seemed to have a good rapport with the students. In the spirit of prayer, speaking directly to the Christ, I asked, "Where did it all go wrong? I believe you were a great spiritual warrior. So why haven't people taken to heart what you taught all those years ago?" I compared the present-day Ireland and Britain to the biblical time of Jesus. I wondered why we had such a hard time struggling to embrace his principles of peace and love. I thought about the similarities between the Roman Empire and the British Empire, The Sanhedrin and the Catholic Church, The Zealots and the Irish Republican Army. When I posed my questions to Jesus, I heard an answer: "Seek and you will find." The words were so crystal clear in my mind that it seemed as if Jesus himself must have whispered them in my ear. This was a defining moment in my life; the beginning of what has been both an adventure and a spiritual quest.

I decided to begin my quest by discovering what the various religions of Northern Ireland have in common. To this end, I attended any number of religious and spiritual services around Belfast. At most of these, I found the message to be pretty much the same: love for God is paramount in our lives, and we should love and respect each other. I read the New Testament and didn't find any teaching that said otherwise. As my seeking picked up momentum, I saw that certain "guidance" was starting to come to me.

For instance, one day in a bookstore in West Belfast I asked for *Cage Eleven*, a book by the politician Gerry Adams. At this time I was trying to get more insight into the thinking of Ireland's political leaders. *Cage Eleven* was usually in stock, the clerk assured me, but neither of us could find it on the shelves. Then just as I was leaving the store, a book fell off one of the shelves we'd been looking on. It was *Cage Eleven*. The clerk handed it to me, saying, "It looks like you were meant to have this book." I agreed. Soon, another book would fall off the shelf in another book shop literally at my feet, and it would turn out to be exactly what I needed to read. The book was *Life after Life* by Raymond A. Moody, which described people's near-death experiences, and life beyond our three-dimensional reality. It seemed quite clear to me that I was receiving help of a higher order.

The book *Life after Life* inspired me to visit a spiritualist church on Malone Avenue. The whole idea of discovering more about what happens when we die fascinated me. I remember thinking, "Wow! Right here in the heart of Belfast, people are openly communicating with the dead!" The congregation was receiving guidance and messages from loved ones who had died — or, as they said, "passed on" — in the same style as many of the "medium" shows on television today. But this was 1988, and there wasn't anything like that on television then.

In one of these services I had an extraordinary thought: "Wouldn't it be wonderful if all those who were involved in killing people in the north of Ireland could come to a church like this. Then those they had killed could communicate with them telepathically. The ones who'd been killed could 'come through' and say, "Hello! I'm still alive you know! Only I'm on a different plane of existence now." And the killers could say, "Well, so you are. Maybe I need to rethink a few things. What am I doing? If the people I kill simply move on to another plane of existence, then maybe I need to look at life differently. Maybe I need to change my strategy.'"" My search was giving me a different perspective on life and death.

My quest continued and expanded to include topics like karma and reincarnation, mediums, and telepathy, spirit guides, angels, extra-terrestrials, and auras. As my focus shifted to these subtle and lofty topics, I began to undergo changes in my personality and perspective. I found that I wasn't arguing as much, and I wasn't getting upset about little things. I felt myself becoming more centered, more compassionate, more accepting of myself and others. My fears began to dissolve. I truly felt a strong spiritual guidance and protection around me. In fact, I was thinking about God quite a bit. At night in my apartment in Belfast, I used to lie in bed and stare at the stars through my skylight feeling in awe of the creation of it all and for the Creator.

I never shared any of this with my friends or family, not because I was afraid of their reaction but because I felt that I was being guided by a higher intelligence, and that my friends and family simply would not understand what I was going through. There were times when I would attend prayer groups to talk to other people who were experiencing some sort of an awakening.

As the conflict and killing continued in Northern Ireland, on the 24th of February 1988 the news reported that two Ulster Defense Regiment (UDR) members, James Cummings and Frederick Starrett, were killed when a remote-controlled bomb was detonated by the IRA in Royal Avenue, Belfast. Five days later two IRA members, Brendan Moley and Brendan Burns, were killed in a premature explosion in County Armagh.

I felt increasingly frustrated with our political leaders as peace, it seemed, was not high on the political agenda. The government spoke of "an acceptable level of violence" but it was my firm belief that life in Ireland was not normal. For me there is no such thing as an "acceptable level of violence." Somehow the violence had to stop. I couldn't add my energy to the negativity of those Irish and British leaders who offered no constructive ideas for resolving the conflict in Ireland. I felt I had to stay positive and open to spirit guidance.

There were also many times when I wanted to express my solidarity with the people of Ireland who desired Irish independence, but many of them were involved in the "armed struggle." I might have understood this approach, but I could never support it. Still, because of my sympathies for "the cause," on March 16th 1988 I found myself attending a triple funeral for three IRA volunteers — Mairead Farrell, Danny McCann, and Sean Savage — one of whom had lived just minutes from my home. These three were killed by a British SAS undercover unit in Gibraltar. Later, it was reported that the IRA were planning to bomb a parade in which a British Army band would be marching. The British shot the IRA members before they had the opportunity to accomplish their mission.

The funeral was attended by thousands of people. At the cemetery Gerry Adams, president of Sinn Féin, the Irish Republican Party, began to speak by the graveside of one of the volunteers. I was standing about twenty yards behind Mr. Adams when suddenly I heard some shots followed by a grenade explosion just a few feet from him. Two more explosions followed as I jumped for cover behind a gravestone. I crouched down motionless as the shots continued. A few seconds later I looked up and as the smoke from the grenades began to fill the air I saw the attacker, a loyalist called Michael Stone, running towards the nearby motorway, shooting at those from the crowd of mourners who were chasing him. He was caught, but not before he had killed three people: twenty-year-old Thomas McErlean, twenty-six-year old John Murray, and thirty-year-old IRA member Kevin Brady, who I later read, had tried to disarm him. Some of the crowd took the attacker away in a car; they were soon intercepted by the police, and he was arrested.

There we were, in a cemetery mourning three deaths, and now there were three more deaths, and many injuries as well, with sirens blaring and vehicles roaring through a place that was supposed to be a quiet sanctuary for the dead and the grieving. It was utter chaos.

For weeks following this madness I looked deep within my heart for ways to help end the suffering of my fellow countrymen and women. Bobby Sands, the first republican prisoner to die on hunger strike, once said, "Everyone, republican or otherwise, has his or her own part to play." I felt that I fell into the "otherwise" category. I felt, true to his words, that my part, my role in supporting peace in Ireland would soon unfold.

By 1992, I felt my soul whisper to me to leave the country and to travel to the United States. Most of the spiritual writers I was getting familiar with were from the USA so I thought that possibly the best way to connect with them and their spiritual message was to travel. At the time I was playing the drums in a rock band, but as much as I loved this job the whisper of my soul got the better of me. I left Belfast for the United States in August 1992, eventually settling in the Boston area.

After acquiring an apartment in Dorchester, Massachusetts, I began to explore the topics of karma and reincarnation. I had already tried unsuccessfully to find a therapist in Belfast trained in the art of past-life regression. I had read that under hypnosis you could recall previous lives; who you were, what you had done, what lessons you had left to learn. I'd visited a popular Irish hypnotist who'd had a lot of success in helping people overcome their addictions. When I asked him if he could retrieve some past-life information for me, he looked at me pityingly and told me that there was no such thing as past lives and that people under hypnosis were just re-experiencing a movie they'd seen at some point earlier in their life. I thanked him for his time but didn't allow his view on this subject to deter me from pursuing the matter.

The second Irish hypnotherapist I saw shared my views on past lives, but as much as she tried to hypnotize me, I just couldn't "go under."

In Boston that November I found a past-life therapist and medium listed in the business directory of the Boston phone book. Her name was Leslie Kiernan and she truly had the gift of vision. On my first visit to her home I was immediately struck by the serenity of her healing and meditation room. The sweet aroma of incense filled the air, and I felt a great peace as I looked at the photographs she displayed of some of the spiritual teachers of history, including The Buddha and Jesus. When Leslie asked me to lie on her healing table she placed some crystals with various healing prosperities on my chest and around my body. As Leslie tuned into the subtle realms she described seeing a Native American standing right beside me as she worked with my aura, the energy field around the physical body. I had believed in spirit guides and guardians for quite some time, and now, finally, I had found someone who seemed to be able to see and talk with them.

Leslie also had a vision of me in a previous life as a tribesman named Tombo, meaning, "Tree of Light." She was so attuned to the spiritual realms that she could see far into my soul's past and into its future. She could communicate telepathically with loved ones who had passed on, and also with spirit guides, angels, and great beings from various spiritual traditions. Along with all of this, Leslie was still totally humble with regards to her gift of mediumship. I realized I had found the person I was looking for. In the telephone book, I had found a "human telephone" to the higher realms of existence.

I had one session after another with Leslie, and much of the information that was channeled through her greatly supported me on my journey over the following eight years. The sessions opened a door to a deeper understanding of my journey for this life. The mystery of my life purpose was becoming clearer.

Chapter 2

Karma

During my time in Boston in the early nineties I made every effort to stay focused on my spiritual path. At times I found the endeavor to be quite challenging, as I was missing my family back in Ireland a lot. I could not separate myself from the Irish struggles either, and I would keep in touch with Irish affairs through the Irish-American newspapers. There seemed to be so much frustration and anger and even despair with the lack of any progress on the political front, but despite this I was still optimistic that change could come.

I was drawn to some new writings on the subject of karma and reincarnation. I had learned that karma is the universal law of cause and effect: every action, every thought, has an equal and opposite reaction. To clarify, "opposite" in this context doesn't mean that love brings hate; it means that when we put love into the universe, then love is what comes back to us from the universe. Whatever we send out into the universe is returned to us; as Jesus puts it," As you sow, so shall you reap."

One book I found that speaks of karma is Ruth Montgomery's *Companions along the Way*. In it, she says that according to ancient mystics, groups of souls that were interconnected in previous lifetimes tend to return to take birth again at approximately the same time and into circumstances that will permit them to continue working out their karmic inter-relationships. Mrs. Montgomery calls this "group karma." It is a great way for God to ensure that people will work on learning to love each other. Unless we're willing to be linked lifetime after lifetime with people we dislike, we have to learn how to rise above our animosities and develop ties of love. This teaching got me thinking about the Irish conflict from a very different perspective. What if all the major Irish and British politicians were karmically tied to each other from other lifetimes? Maybe this lifetime was yet another opportunity for them to resolve their differences and help create peace between Britain and Ireland. This consideration was not really a concept I was ready to share with anyone, of course. It just didn't feel like the right time. Still, I was fascinated by what Ruth Montgomery and her guides had to say. Her books were allowing me to see myself more as an actor in a karmic play, with a role that was gradually unfolding and revealing itself.

While going deeper into the subject matter of karma, Ruth Montgomery makes it clear that everything she writes comes to her from personal spirit guides, whom she describes as Light Beings from the higher realms of existence. According to her guides, souls in the spirit world are drawn together by the power of their feelings for each other. This might be mutual empathy and like-mindedness, and it might be envy, animosity, or even hatred. For the most part, in the spirit world there isn't the kind of disharmony that we encounter on the physical plane. But those souls who have met again and again in their various incarnations have great attraction for each other, and some of these connections are negative in nature. The spirit guides point out that it is good to break any negative ties and that the best way to do this is by returning good for evil, turning the other cheek, and learning to recognize the beneficial qualities of others, so that our anger and hatred may die out. Then negative bonds can be dissolved or can even turn into connections of love. I find that this subtle understanding of my interactions with others can be particularly useful when I encounter people with whom I am not now in harmony. It always helps to remember this perspective — and the practical matter of meeting certain souls again and again in order to work things out.

Ruth Montgomery communicated with her spirit guides through the process of mental telepathy called automatic writing. She reported that at the same time every morning, she would sit at her typewriter, place her hands on the keyboard, repeat an affirmation, and then listen carefully. She might have to wait a bit, but eventually words would pour through her mind, and then she would type everything she heard. Mrs Montgomery first encountered psychic phenomena in the 1960s, when she was a nationally-syndicated news columnist and a White House press correspondent. She had covered Washington for twenty years, from the time of president Franklin D. Roosevelt through that of president Lyndon B. Johnson. In the beginning she was highly skeptical of these telepathic communications from beyond our three-dimensional world. But she listened, she recorded, and she published what she heard, and thus went on to become a best-selling author of books on paranormal topics: reincarnation, extraterrestrial visitation, life after death, and so on — fifteen books in all.

I returned again and again to Ruth's book *Companions along the Way*, as her revelations were so enlightening. Ruth included an account of the Rosenberg espionage case by the attorney Louis Nizer entitled *The Implosion Conspiracy*. This very astute man observes that there is a cluster phenomenon in human history that defies logical explanation. What happens is this: at infrequent periods in history several geniuses will appear, and often they will know each other. Their fame will last through centuries, and then another cluster of transcendent, talented people will appear and they will dominate the landscape. Some of the clusters Mr. Rizer identifies are Shakespeare and Bacon; Leonardo da Vinci and Verrocchio with Michelangelo and Raphael. In music there was Mozart, Beethoven, Haydn, and Schubert; then a century later came Brahms, Liszt, and Schumann. In the philosophical field there was Voltaire, Rousseau, and Diderot. In jurisprudence, Holmes, Brandeis, and Hughes all sat on the Supreme Court at the same time. And in the political arena, many have pondered the extraordinary coincidence of such towering statesmen as Thomas Jefferson, George Washington, John Adams, Alexander Hamilton, Benjamin Franklin, and others being present simultaneously at the birth of the United States.

Was this luck, asks Ruth Montgomery, or had these remarkable souls decided to come back together again in order to establish a free nation as an example to all mankind? Ruth quotes her spirit guides as saying that nothing is an accident and that groups of souls return again and again to develop their talents to the highest possible point, whether that talent is for writing, painting, music, mathematics, statesmanship, and so on.

I came across one of Shakespeare's most often quoted lines — "All the world's a stage, and all the men and women merely players" — in a context that supported my new perspective on karma, reincarnation, and humanity playing specific roles in the play of life. Frederick Von Mierers, the teacher of a course known as "The Eternal Values," explains that we can visualize this beautiful planet as a stage, each individual on it an actor in a play, and God the director of that play. At our death, the end of our life's role, we return backstage. No matter how we've performed, at the end of each performance we can review our role, with the help of the director and his assistants. Then, whether or not we've earned applause, the director gives us the opportunity to take on a new role — a role in which we can try to accomplish that with which we'd had difficulty in our previous performance and, sometimes, where we can have a positive effect on the play itself. We have the opportunity to return again and again to the stage until we've mastered our trade. And then we can move on to greater roles in the universal play that we call life.

This deeper understanding of karma created a further shift in my understanding. I began to feel more and more that part of my "role" in this lifetime was to look for some way to convince the politicians about the necessity of creating peace in Ireland. I began to feel that this was my karma, carried over from a previous life, and that this karma could only be resolved in my soul when peace was achieved in Ireland.

Chapter 3

The Past-Life Sessions

As I contemplated how I could connect with those all-important Irish and British politicians, I returned to my good friend Leslie hoping to receive more information on my own personal karmic purpose. I felt that the more I understood who I was, the greater confidence I would have in approaching the political leaders. The spiritual awakening I was experiencing reaffirmed to me that *all* people were created equal. Why should I fear the politicians, or anyone else for that matter?

As I rode the bus and train to Leslie's home in Lexington I thought about how she communicated with the guides. I knew that it was different from the automatic writing done by Ruth Montgomery, but only in the most superficial way; the basic process was actually quite similar. To my knowledge all mediums follow certain steps in their work: they quieten their minds, offer some form of prayer or affirmation, and then listen carefully to whatever they may hear mentally. Whether they then record the telepathic message in writing or repeat it aloud is a minor matter. Some mediums, or channelers as they are sometimes known, might even see or feel the presence of the spirit guides or angels communicating through them. Again, for me this is not the most important consideration. What matters most in telepathic communications, I feel, is the message itself, the wisdom that comes from beings that exist on a plane more subtle than our own.

Channeling, I discovered through Leslie, was not just a modern phenomenon, it was an ancient practice. Some of the Earth's oldest civilizations — the ancient Egyptians and the Native Americans to name two — were masters of the telepathic science of channeling. For the Native Americans, these traditions continue to this very day. In Native American culture, the shamans and medicine men have historically held positions of great respect, and it's evident that they channel guidance from the spirit world in their rituals.

Books on shamanic practice say that years of preparation are necessary before a shaman can begin his work and that most shamans precede any channeling session with fasting and prayer. It's my understanding that arduous preparation is a necessity for channels, no matter what their tradition or personal gifts may be. This preparation is a healing, a cleansing of the channel on all levels: physical, emotional, mental, and spiritual. It makes sense that to be a good conduit, a channel must be clear. To be a clear channel of Light, love, and higher intelligence, the channeler, medium, or automatic writer must be mentally and emotionally grounded, and must be able to put their ego and preconceptions aside. If the medium's ego gets involved, then communications could be distorted and the messages from the spirit world could be misleading or even inaccurate. The clearer the channel, the clearer the message.

Through all my early sessions with Leslie I realized that the most important thing about a channel, that you won't know until you've done a session with them, is the nature of the message they carry. High spiritual guidance is always positive and uplifting, and it has only your best interests at heart. I wanted to open this possibility of subtle exploration of spirituality to other people who, like me, wrestle with questions about who we are and why we're here.

When I finally reached Leslie's house I found her outside in the garden watering her plants. Leslie loved her garden and treated it with great reverence. "Hi Paul! How are you?" she said cheerfully, "Let me just finish up."

"No problem, Leslie! Your garden looks beautiful by the way. I don't know how you keep it so well."

"Ah Paul," she replied, "There's nothing to it. A little tenderness, that's all."

As we made our way inside Leslie's home I was struck as always by the peace and serenity of this sacred haven she called home. I also found it amusing that, among the various pictures of the great saints and masters that hung on her walls, Leslie reserved space for several Keanu Reeves photographs. Yes indeed. As well as being a gifted healer and channel, Leslie had a bit of a crush on the actor.

After moving into the meditation room we prepared for our session. Our sessions usually began with Leslie and I sitting upright facing each other, focusing first on our breathing and then going into meditation. At some point Leslie would start giving voice to whatever she was hearing telepathically. It was clear to me when the words she spoke were not hers. I say this because the rhythm of speech wasn't her natural rhythm. Also, after a session she always had very little recollection of what had just come through her.

As I sat with Leslie I felt totally protected and sure in the knowledge that highly-conscious beings from the higher dimensional realities were watching over us both, ready and willing to guide, inform, and serve the common goal of supporting an awakening humanity. I also thought about Leslie's hand in all this work and how much more acceptable to society the healing arts were during these times on earth. I thought about a time when humanity thought the world was flat. Then along came a few expansive and open-minded souls who were willing to explore the revolutionary possibility that the world was indeed a sphere. These pioneers were scorned, impoverished, even executed by the authorities of their day. And yet now we know for a fact that their suppositions about the shape of the Earth were right and that it was humankind that needed to be corrected.

The same could be said for some Biblical prophecies. At the time the prophets made these extraordinary predictions, there were some who believed them, but many others who didn't, who thought they were the meaningless rantings of lunatics. Many of these prophets of old were really just channelers. And just as these ancient seers were channels of Light and higher knowledge, so there are channels today, like Leslie, whose awareness was so heightened that they were able to receive and convey divine knowledge.

With regard to the messages I received through Leslie, I would simply hold the communications in my awareness and see what happened and how I felt about them over time. I observed that any predictions I received would generally prove to be accurate.

During this particular session I was just referring to, in early 1993, I felt a great sense of peace and stillness in the room as Leslie and I sat facing each other. Leslie then pressed the record button on her tape recorder. She would record almost every session we had so that I could reflect and study the communications again at home. After sitting quietly in meditation for a short while, Leslie invoked the guidance and protection of the Light Beings. After only a few moments, she began to "speak" in a loving, yet authoritative tone:

"Greetings in the Light! This is Quacate. (pronounced Quah-chee)I am not your guardian angel but your spiritual guide, like an angel. I chose to teach you because we have known one another before. We have been brothers and sisters. I have completed my lifetimes on Earth at this time, and it is now part of my commitment, my growth, to work with souls I have known on the Earth plane. I chose this Light body to show you, and this name, because the lifetime we knew together in this form was particularly good and there was a strong affinity between us.

In this lifetime, Paul, you are learning to accept leadership with humility. You are learning to be a servant of others by speaking of Light, and you have come to purify your ego. You are part of the Brotherhood of Light and also what is considered the One Brotherhood. Within the One Brotherhood, you are part of - shall we say - tribes, or tribal energies, that overlay and overlap. The capacity is lodged within you to recognize the multi-dimensions of yourself and the others around you. You are also playing in a team that will break down the boundaries created by differences, and yet remain respectful of distinctions. You will connect with many group energies, which, in the Aquarian Age, are uniting as one. You are becoming aware of the new consciousness and information that is coming into this dimension. You are becoming aware somewhat ahead of some and somewhat behind others.

What this means is that as you come into this information, you then pass it on to others who are not yet aware. Truly, all souls on Earth are participating in some way.

And so you have chosen to awaken and to understand many things, to re-understand and to newly-learn things with the guidance and help of many who have gone on before you, including those in other dimensions, such as the Brotherhood of Light that speaks to you now. We are here to teach you and guide you, and it is recommended that you continue to speak with us. We feel your love and your prayers, and we love and appreciate you. When you broadcast this love, it strengthens the connection between us. It is very important on the Earth plane that people open themselves to listen to the higher consciousness that comes from their own higher self or from their spiritual guides."

What a beautiful start to the sessions, I thought. Quacate was basically affirming to me that I was on the right track when I chose to "broadcast" the message of love from my guides and guardians, whom he would later refer to as the Family of Light. When there came an opportunity for me to ask a question, I didn't hesitate. I knew exactly what I wanted to know. As I said before, I've never regarded myself as a religious person, and yet for years I'd been extremely interested in the appearances of the Mother Mary. Since my childhood I'd been deeply moved by a film called *Song of Bernadette*, which was about a peasant girl from Lourdes, France, who received visitations from Mother Mary in 1858. To this day I'm still touched by the movie every time I see it. In Ireland I would attend prayer groups and apparition slide shows, discreetly sitting in a back corner where I could listen to the Mary apparition stories without being too visible myself. The movie *Jesus of Nazareth* also had a strong impact on me as a child; I felt as if I were watching something very familiar to me. So, I asked:

"Quacate; I'm not sure why, because I'm not really a religious man, but there have been many times in my life when I would think about Mother Mary. I would experience her as "the mother of compassion" and my heart would melt on hearing stories of her apparitions. Can you tell why I have these feelings?"

Quacate replied,

"Mother Mary has appeared to you more than once. You may have not realized this was her name, but you did experience her as angelic. One of these visitations was a spiritual experience. You felt the awareness of a higher consciousness. This happened in the time you now know as Biblical, when you were around Jesus himself. You experienced Mother Mary as an angel. This was a profoundly moving event as your own energy was brought into the higher state. This was a significant spiritual experience for you in that lifetime.

Earlier in Egypt, where you knew Samaria to be, before the life of Jesus, you were also connected to the consciousness you call Mother Mary. A third visitation took place when you lived as a knight in the time of King Arthur. When you knelt in prayer, she would often come to you to guide you and speak to you."

Quacate's words affirmed to me that even though the soul memory of my past lives had remained hidden from me, the affinity that I felt — in this case for Mother Mary and for Jesus — had been held in my subconscious. This is why I had been so drawn to Mother Mary and why the scene around Jesus seemed familiar to me. I felt incredibly moved by this revelation as my eyes began to well up.

I felt in that moment that it must be that way for all of us. We are drawn to certain people, places, objects, vocations, and experiences, because they are familiar to us from our past lives. Quacate explained to me that the experiences of all our lifetimes are recorded deep in our consciousness. Everything we have ever been, known, done, felt, in any lifetime affects our experience in this present lifetime. This is not to say that the experiences of our past lifetimes are a part of our conscious memory. For the most part, we live through the destiny we have created for ourselves without consciously knowing why we've created it. We do this so that we can, finally, learn the lessons we failed to learn before. It was our soul's purpose to resolve all our accrued karma and to live as fully-conscious beings of love.

With regards to my homeland, I learned that my strong desire to see peace between Ireland and Britain also probably stemmed from a previous lifetime. Our desires and goals were motive forces in our lives, and so these desires came forward from one lifetime to the next until they were satisfied or resolved. Quacate explained to me that it isn't important to consciously recall every instant in which karma is created; if it were, we would have time for little else. What was important was to acknowledge our passions and to find ways of addressing them. He pointed out to me that my concern, my thoughts, and especially my feelings — the very love that I was sending to my homeland — made a difference in resolving the enmity that so disturbed me. This bit of information was a revelation for me. If the thoughts and prayers of just one person can make a difference in bringing peace to a nation, then what would be the effect of thousands upon thousands of prayers sent forth for the sake of peace? It was my strong belief that the heavenly realms could hear every prayer and in time these prayers would have impact.

After leaving Leslie's house I felt tremendous gratitude for all that I received from Quacate. As the sessions continued and I learned more and more of my past lifetimes, I would keep asking myself, who am I? I could feel that the answer was within my reach. Jesus once said, "The Kingdom of Heaven is within," To me, those words mean that the highest love and knowledge lay within me — and also within each one of us. I could see that it wasn't necessary for everyone to know where, and what, and who they were in their previous lifetimes, but that it is necessary for each of us to recognize our divine essence. This concept became easier for me to understand the more I learned through the sessions about my collective past — how I had lived near Bethlehem with a wife and family, was deeply touched once when my wife and I bowed at a sacred site of the crucifixion in Jerusalem, and how I was touched by Jesus' spiritual power in that lifetime; how I was married to that same soul in the medieval Kingdom of Arthur; how I worshipped the Buddha both as a householder in Japan and a monk in Tibet; how in India I was the widow of a man killed in a cave by a tiger, and in Atlantis I was a priestess who worked with sound and light; how I worshiped Ra, the sun god, in Egypt; how I was a shaman, a medicine man, a meditator. My soul had chosen to incarnate in many forms, identities, different places, and life situations. As I asked for information about one lifetime after another, I began to understand what my guides were telling me: that no matter what our physical "garment" may be in the moment, we are all experiencing lessons in the school of life. In this school there was only one course of study: love.

The information that poured forth from Quacate and the higher-conscious beings of the "Family of Light" over the next few years continued to surprise me and inspire me. But, of course, there were also times I had to take a reality check and ask myself "Is this really happening to me?" At times I would be reluctant to share the stories, as I believed that most people wouldn't understand – and would even think I was crazy. Eventually I accepted that being called the crazy one from time to time was part of my life path, and that sharing my truth was the most important thing. While learning some of the details about my past lives from the Family of Light I would be granted a better grasp of karma and reincarnation, which greatly assisted me in understanding why I was back in this world as Paul Gavan. I could see that there was still much to learn, and yet Quacate and the Family of Light would assure me that all the knowledge I needed was already within me. Whenever I looked within, through meditation or self-inquiry, I would find what I needed. This was *my* truth. When I asked, the answers were revealed to me — exactly as much as I needed to know at the exact time that I needed to know it.

Chapter 4

Jesus, UFOs, and Ireland

In my next few sessions with Leslie, the Family of Light would remind me of the importance of trusting my own soul. They would say that everything I needed was encoded in my heart. And so, inspired by them, I dug deeper into the principles of spirituality. A few months earlier I had read the book *Mary's Message to the World* which carried the words of Mother Mary, channeled through Annie Kirkwood. Annie received both visions and messages from Mother Mary telling of certain Earth changes that were going to take place at some point in the not-too-distant future. Mary predicted that a new era of peace would manifest on Earth and that UFOs would become a common sight. This UFO prediction surprised me as I never really associated the subject with spirituality before. And so I began to explore the connection. I wondered how celestial beings might be influencing Earth life in 1993; it made sense to me that our Creator would not limit His creation to one planet and one intelligent species. Why indeed should there not be countless souls roaming the universe, each with its own design and blueprint for life? I believed that most people on our planet would be open to the possibility that other intelligent life forms co-exist with us in the universe but unfortunately it seemed most media and governments were covering up the many reports of UFO sightings. Why was this so, I wondered?

In March 1993 I needed to fly to London for an interview for my US Green Card. After a successful interview I flew back to Belfast for a visit. While back in Ireland I found that the political situation there was more or less the same as it had been for some years. Another bomb had recently exploded in Warrington, England, with the result that two young boys were killed and yet another family was devastated. Saddened by this news and the state of affairs I took some time to walk the Black Mountain, which overlooks the city of Belfast. The view was stunning. I could see Belfast Lough and the Harland and Wolff shipyard, where the Titanic was built. The beauty of Belfast was so evident, and yet all I could think of was the struggles and suffering of the people of this city. I prayed once again that the struggle would end. I continued contemplating Mother Mary's message, especially her words on UFOs, and the possible reasons for her increasing number of appearances to people throughout the planet. I thought about her son, Jesus. I thought about how he must have witnessed so much suffering under the oppressive Roman Empire during his time on Earth. I thought about the great compassion he must have had for the masses who probably felt powerless against the great might of the Romans. While contemplating this I felt deep within my being that the energy of Jesus was watching over me as I sat on top of the mountain trying to figure out my role and the role of spirituality in Irish politics. I felt I could play a part but I needed the wisdom and guidance of Jesus, Mary, Quacate, and the higher realms. And so again I asked within to be aligned with the Divine Will as I made my way back down the mountain to my family home.

Not long after returning to Boston in April 1993, I came across the book *Talks with Christ* by the renowned scientist and educator Charles H. Hapgood. As testimony to Professor Hapgood's work, in the preface of another of his books, *Earth's Shifting Crust*, Albert Einstein praised the work as being of great importance to everything that is related to the Earth's surface. *Talks with Christ* recounts a series of talks from Jesus through the medium Elwood Babbitt. In *Talks with Christ*, Charles Hapgood posed his questions, and Elwood Babbitt channeled the answers to these questions from Jesus. Mr. Babbitt was in a deep trance as he spoke; the session was similar to my communications with the spirit world through Leslie. I had read any number of accounts of mediums communicating with loved ones, or spirit guides who had passed on from this world, but this was the first time I'd heard about someone I recognized as a great soul communicating through a medium. Of course, I thought of Mother Mary as a great soul, but I felt that she had appeared to people and spoken with them in visions and in response to prayer. Until this moment, I'd never thought of that as "channeling." Possibly because the method Professor Hapgood used to communicate with Jesus was so close to what I myself had used with a channel, I began to see that all of these inspired works are, in fact, channeling.

Talks with Christ included eighteen conversations with Jesus which took place over eleven years, beginning on December 3, 1967. As I read this book I could feel a great power behind the written words that seemed to cause a deep level of transformation within me. My mind and heart had now accepted that channeling any spirit, anywhere, in the physical or spiritual worlds, was possible. Through prayer and meditation, I now believed that humanity could communicate with any entity it so desired. I believed that all we needed was faith in our ability to make the connection.

Even though I was now feeling a deeper connection to Jesus, I was also feeling very lonely after once again leaving my entire family and my friends back in Ireland. Although the feeling was quite strong, I never confused loneliness with being alone, isolated, or bereft. For I knew now that the Family of Light was with me and that I was - in the nicest sense - being watched over, protected, and guided.

Early one evening, as I was sitting on a hilltop near my apartment in Savin Hill, Dorchester, marveling in the beauty of the sunset, I noticed three huge lights in a triangle formation high in the twilight sky. At first I thought it might be three helicopters, but the lights disappeared then reappeared a few seconds later, all blinking in unison. This continued for about ten minutes, and then I saw what looked like two military planes take off from the area of Boston's Logan Airport and head straight for the three huge lights. At that point the three lights simply disappeared. The military planes were still patrolling the sky when I returned to my apartment. I thought about these three huge lights in their triangular formation for some time. As I had seen them after reading Mother Mary's messages on

UFOs, and after further sessions with Leslie and the Family of Light, I took this as a sign that whoever was occupying this "UFO" knew who I was, and that these beings of a higher order were acknowledging this by making their presence felt — and felt, it seemed, by more people than just me. Incredibly, within two years, I was to have another similar experience.

On August 18th, 1995, as I returned home to my apartment, then in Arlington, I was met by my roommate, Susan, who was just about to leave for a trip to Vermont.

"Paul! You need to call your brother in Ireland. He said it's an emergency."

I wasn't really sure what to make of Susan's message. I had never received an emergency message from anyone in my family before so I thought it was a prank from my brother. Still, I went inside, picked up the phone and dialed home. As soon as my brother answered I knew something was not right.

"Paul," he said. I just knew what he was about to say next was not going to be good news. After a brief pause, as if to give me a moment to settle myself, he simply said, "Mom died this morning." Nothing could have prepared me for these words. I had not seen my mother in two and a half years, since the time of my US Green Card interview. I had talked with her on the phone just six days previously and everything seemed fine. I truly felt that it was only a matter of time before I would return home to see her again. With tears beginning to flow down my cheeks I told my brother that I would be on the next available flight home, which would turn out to be two days later. Three thousand miles away from family, I began to wander the streets in a state of shock. Confused and very angry with God, as I didn't believe this could be part of His plan, I soon arrived at the nearby Spy Pond. I slowly sat down by the water and looked up at the clear night sky. Just then I noticed what looked like a bright light, moving across the sky at great speed. At first I thought it was a shooting star, but every few seconds it moved in a triangular pattern then continued on its way. I watched it until it was out of sight, a period of several minutes. It was clear to me that a light that made these sort of maneuvers was not of this world. I suddenly felt a strong reassuring presence around me, as if someone was trying to get my attention and tell me that everything was going to be alright and that my mother was in good hands. This celestial "sign" was yet another reminder to me that in my most difficult and darkest times I was never alone.

Back in the summer of 1993, soon after my first UFO experience, I began to say goodbye to my old lifestyle. My roommates might have thought my lifestyle — my interests, my preferred reading material — a bit odd, but I didn't care. What mattered to me was not how people saw me; it was how well I could follow my inner guidance, strength, and courage. As my mind returned to thoughts of the Irish struggle I felt that if we, the people, were not happy with the way our politicians were handling their responsibilities, then we had a duty to let them know. I believed what was needed were open-minded leaders with an ability to think "outside the box" in their approach to finding a resolution to the conflict. I prayed that some of our current leaders would have the wisdom to engage in this kind of visionary approach.

In the Seven Stars bookstore, in Cambridge Massachusetts, I discovered yet another book that claimed to channel the words of Jesus through the process of telepathic communication. The book was *New Teachings for an Awakening Humanity* by Virginia Essene. This book also explained that humanity was not alone in the universe, that the planet Earth was coming back to a higher frequency of love, and that those people who choose peace will be co-creators in a cosmic process. After reading the book, with its direct account from The Christ on what humanity needed to do to ensure its survival on this planet, I felt an immediate urge to share the book with two men, Sinn Féin President Gerry Adams and John Hume, leader of the Social Democratic Labor Party (SDLP). Mr. Adams and Mr. Hume had been involved in private talks on finding a way forward in the Irish/British conflict. I believed that Mr. Hume and Adams were the open-minded leaders I had been praying for due to their recent genuine efforts to see the conflict resolved. I felt without a doubt that the channeled messages from Jesus, particularly his chapter on 'Guidelines for Scientists, the Military, and Governments,' were directed at such leaders as Mr. Adams and Mr. Hume. To me the book represented a golden opportunity for these two leaders to consider that the highest spiritual authorities watched over us from what The Christ called the "Heavenly Realms," unbeknown to most of humanity, and would support the search for peace in our world. The book was no doubt an "outside the box" influence and yet it absolutely made sense. We were being told by the Heavenly Realms that we were not alone in the universe and that what happened here on earth affected life elsewhere in the cosmos, hence the importance and necessity of creating peace in our world.

And so, from my apartment in Savin Hill in early August, 1993, I sat down to write my letter to Gerry Adams. I wrote with an authority that I believed came from an absolute faith that the Christ energy was right there with me, guiding me. I also wrote with a firm conviction that my letter would, without a shadow of a doubt, reach Gerry Adams. This was based on the assurances given by Jesus in the book that all who chose to be co-creators of peace would be supported by the Heavenly Realms in this endeavor. I felt that my role was simply to be the messenger through which higher celestial intelligence could be shared.

After preparing my letter to Mr. Adams, which included a second copy of the New Teachings book which I had asked that he share with John Hume, I took the opportunity to visit Leslie for a session. It was in this session that The Family of Light revealed to me that that there would soon be a dramatic change in Ireland. They said that there would be a process, that peace would come to Ireland within the next few years, and that I would have a part to play in it. The session was extremely emotional for me. For the first time in my life I experienced an incredible joy through the prediction that there would soon be peace in my homeland. And so, with gratitude to the Family of Light for giving me the confidence I needed, I sent the package containing *New Teaching for an Awakening Humanity*, with its critical contents and call for co-creating peace, to Gerry Adams. I felt that this action was indeed related to my part in the process of which the Family of Light spoke.

Chapter 5

The Ashtar Command

In the fall of 1993, as I continued my work as a painter, I was still thinking constantly about the messages from the Christ. I contemplated God's vast creation and Jesus' explanation of the many life forms that existed in our universe besides humanity. How could humanity call itself "intelligent life" when we knew so very little about the universe around us? By opening up to other realities in the vastness of creation wouldn't we be able to better understand the universe – and ourselves too?

With all these thoughts playing in my mind, my understanding of the UFO phenomenon took another giant leap forward after I discovered a channel by the name of Tuella, whose real name was Thelma Terrell. Tuella was recognized in UFO circles as the primary channel for the Ashtar Command, a group of celestial beings whose leader is known as Ashtar. One of the goals of the Ashtar Command, according to Tuella, was to support humanity's shift into a higher dimensional cosmic reality of love and Light. The Family of Light had also referred to this transformational shift. They said that increasing numbers of people would be coming into this awareness and would be communicating directly with celestial beings, like the Ashtar Command. According to the Command, the intergalactic vehicles we call UFOs were not roaming Earth's skies just for fun but were here to support humanity through this cosmic shift as part of a divine plan from our Creator. The Ashtar Command also informed Tuella that Christ Jesus was well known to celestial intelligences throughout the universe and that his service to God extended far beyond his role as Lord of this planet.

I found Tuella's channeled communications on behalf of the Ashtar Command to be incredibly enlightening, and yet at the same time very practical. Much of what they conveyed was a call for each of us to awaken to our true nature, our divine origins, and to accept that this cosmic transition into a new age of enlightenment was our divine destiny.

During a session with Leslie I asked the Family of Light if they could reveal a little more on the Ashtar Command. This was their response:

"The Ashtar Command is connected to Light, to all Light, and is the highest form of intelligence. The Command and all its components are very interested in the play-out of the plan here on Earth. Let us say there is an investment of love, time, and energy, and a desire to help earthlings to preserve the beauty of this planet and not to destroy it. It is like a divine game that is being played out. The Earth is a school of learning for souls to evolve, and it is the plane where,

as a result of this growth, karma is resolved. At the end of this game we expect the Light to flash brightly and fill all beings with ecstasy. Every being in the Ashtar Command is also in a growth process at a different level. This includes the beings you call Light Beings, spirit guides, and angels. It is one force with many components that work together to heal you all. You could say that those of the Command take on assignments that are well suited to their need for growth and thus well suited to your need at the time. There is a constant communication of intelligence and Light. This is not so easy for you to perceive, as there is so much blockage in communication and energy on the plane where you are currently living. The higher dimension of you understands this complete open connection, and you long for it, but you have chosen to participate in this game at this level. Do not misunderstand the use of the word "game." It is not a negative. It is a descriptive word chosen at this time. The beings that are channeling through and bringing Light to this dimension are influencing what happens. This is grace being focused to and brought to situations as they play out. In other words, without this it would be much more chaotic and painful than it is at this time. We are here to heal the minds of all, the One Mind, and while any component of this mind is unconscious or sick, the whole suffers and so we all work together to create oneness and perfection."

The Family of Light continued with more personal information for both Leslie and I.

"Both you and Leslie are awake enough to be choosing to be channels of Light. The way that you bring in the Light will evolve as you evolve

and your own personal karma is softened as you bring Light to others through yourself. That is all that is truly important, as you were saying earlier. The most important thing is that there is Light, and you are Light, the Light of the world. Many souls of the One Soul are in great pain and fear and it is your choice to bring Light and grace to yourself really. This is the greatest tenet, loving one another. And so when you feel called to send messages of love, it is wonderful in any way that you do this. Also, Paul, you have certain guides working with you who have a common interest and common goal and feel called to send this energy to Ireland where things have definitely taken a turn, shall we say, inward to the Light. This will be a process. The important thing is that direction has shifted due to the work of many Light beings. It is all unfolding perfectly."

Again the Family of Light referred to an Irish "process" and also stated that there were other guides with a common interest in Ireland. I felt that maybe these other guides were the ones that were with me back in Belfast when the book I wanted caught my attention by falling from the shelf. I asked my guides about this. They replied:

We will answer your question about the past event and the book falling from the shelf. Indeed, it fell and, although not exactly making contact with you physically, you were hit in the third eye and the crown [chakra, at the top of the head]. Relating this story as an example of guidance, spiritually, will work because truly you were guided by the Light in that moment and that will communicate."

I asked for more guidance and an opportunity to share the messages from the Ashtar Command with influential people. And once again the opportunity presented itself.

I had read an article in the *Irish Voice* newspaper about a fundraiser peace initiative, which was dedicated to promoting peace in Northern Ireland. I was moved by the organizations efforts in promoting peace so I contacted one of their representatives through the *Irish Voice* newspaper. He was in New York City promoting the project. As we spoke on the phone I found him to very engaging and open to talk with me regarding peace initiatives. We arranged to meet in the Sin-é pub in New York City the following day.

That evening I took the fifteen-minute walk from my apartment to the JFK Library in Dorchester, where I did most of my letter writing. On the way it occurred to me that I could write another letter to Gerry Adams, include the Ashtar Command messages, and then ask the peace activist to forward it to Mr. Adams if possible. I felt that given his current profile as peace activist he would stand a good chance of getting the package to Mr. Adams. Before I began writing the letter I invoked the guidance and support of the Family of Light. While writing I felt a strong urge to include a request that Mr. Adams forward the message of the Ashtar Command to the Army Council of the IRA (Irish Republican Army). I explained in the letter that we had to work with our protestant brothers and sisters to bring about a resolution to the conflict. I requested that we heed the call of the Ashtar Command for world peace. "Let us not forget, but forgive," I wrote in recognition that republicans had also suffered as a result of the conflict. I recognized the Army Council's power of forgiveness, and that of all parties affected by the conflict, was necessary in order to move forward in search of a peaceful resolution.

The next day I boarded the bus to New York City. After arriving at the Sin-é pub I was eventually greeted by the peace activist who was also accompanied by another peace representative. We quickly settled down to the serious subject at hand - peace in Ireland. I gave him several packages all containing the message of the Ashtar Command requesting that he; if possible, share them with various people in Ireland. I explained the contents and also asked if he could forward one particular package to Gerry Adams. He replied that he would certainly try.

After our meeting I made my way back to Boston confident that the Family of Light would continue to support all those involved in the cause of peace. A few weeks later I also sent the message of the Ashtar Command to the loyalist leaders including the Combined Loyalist Military Command (CLMC). Armed with the knowledge that I was supported and guided by the Light, over the following months and years I continued to send out the Ashtar Command's appeal to more than three dozen people who I felt had the personal will and the political or cultural position to make a difference, especially in the interests of peace. From 1993 through 1996 I sent copies to a US senator, congressmen, ambassadors, church leaders, and to representatives of the Northern Irish political parties. I received some prompt and gracious replies thanking me for the books and messages. **In 1996 I also received an unofficial acknowledgement from a senior Sinn Féin political party representative that he was indeed**

familiar with the Ashtar Command. I had a firm faith that the messages and request of the Ashtar Command would reach the right people at the right time. I trusted that the powerful spiritual message and energies that flowed through every word of the *New Teachings* book and the Ashtar Command messages would move the political readers to action, based on the urgency of the Spiritual Hierarchy's appeal for peace. I prayed that all those involved in the conflict in Northern Ireland would accept that we all shared this island and we all needed to act as responsible caretakers of it, as ultimately it belonged to our Creator. Surely all our leaders recognized this? Also, surely they could consider the power of these telepathically-communicated words from some of the greatest souls of all time, including Jesus. Recognizing this love for Jesus that so many had, I asked the Family of Light to comment on their knowledge of this beloved being, loved and worshipped by millions. They spoke the following words:

"The awareness of Jesus the Christ increases on this plane as does the Light at this time. Jesus is with all of you like a light shining the way always. Your ability to experience this Light is ever increasing. There is increasingly more peace on Earth, and the Light workers are intensifying their focus on all planes to bring about the divine plan. It is also a very challenging time as old energy patterns and karma are purified most intensely, especially over this winter. Focus on going within to the inner Light is important always and especially this winter. Quacate and many others are present here to assist in this communication. The Ashtar Command and the Light Beings of the Family of Light all wish to acknowledge your request for information.

The book, Ashtar, will support you and help you maintain contact with the Light Command. The Light Command comes to you in many forms, many ways. It is the one Light ... The process of opening, purifying, and awakening to the Light continues and each session supports and helps along this process. Jesus always took a very direct route and worked in the highest way for elevation and healing in the situation at hand. He simply worked with the Light to transform energy. He is a master of energy and teaches this continually to those who would learn and listen. Truly Jesus works through each of you to stimulate the healing power. It is a matter of allowing healing to happen, embracing the Light and the love that is available, and humbly praying, asking, and receiving. So whatever the tool, style, technique, or form, this is not relevant. What is relevant is the love and the Light you are able to access, draw to you, and hold. It is the love, this energy of Light that heals."

And so, ultimately, with the support of the great Light Beings, we, including our political leaders, had the power to embrace this love, this Light, and heal not only ourselves, but our country, and our entire world. Would we eventually rise to the challenge? I believed the answer was a resounding "YES."

Chapter 6

Holding the Vibration
of Love and Light

In March 1994 I had begun working in a school for the blind. This employment taught me much about service to humanity, about myself, and about my own shortfalls. The first time I had walked through the entrance to the school, for my initial job interview in December 1993, I marveled at the beauty of the landscape with its snow-covered trees and buildings. A tower stood majestically high above all the other buildings with people, some blind with canes, and some in wheelchairs, making their way to and from the tower building. It struck me that this school was different to any I had ever seen before. As I made my way to an adjacent building in the Deaf Blind department I met an Irish acquaintance named Rory who worked at the school. We had previously arranged to meet as he planned on escorting me to his supervisor named Molly, for the interview.

"She should be around here somewhere," he said. "Let's try the dining room."

We eventually caught up with Molly in the dining room as she carried out her daily ritual of checking in with her supervisory staff. As I spoke with her I noticed her smiling and nodding at me quite a bit. When I asked her a question and she continued to smile and nod at me I realized that, like most Americans at the time, she hardly understood a word I said due to my thick Irish accent. I was grateful though because the words Molly did understand were enough to convince her that I was the right man for the job.

After working as a drummer back in Belfast I felt like my new job in working with children with special needs was like stepping into another life. During my early days working in the school for the blind I learned a great deal in the areas of patience, tolerance, and compassion. One student, named Brandon, loved to watch the movie character *Mr. Bean. Mr. Bean* is a comedy show about a man whose whole life is made up of one funny situation after another. He hardly talks, but words are not needed. Because Brandon laughed hysterically at this character I would imitate Mr. Bean. He smiled and laughed as I jokingly walked into doors or tripped over objects lying on the floor. Brandon was totally dependent on his staff to feed him, clothe him, and transport him around in his wheelchair. He used a communication device as he couldn't talk verbally. Brandon would sometimes get frustrated because he couldn't help his staff more with regards his own feeding and changing but I never once saw him angry with anyone. Even though he was a young, twenty one-year-old man, totally dependent on other people for his every physical need, he was still a great influence on me.

A few years later, after moving to another department in the school, another student came to the school. His name was Johnny. Johnny was born with a rare chromosome disorder. When he was born the doctors said his time on Earth would be brief. Johnny was an incredibly strong boy though. When I first met him I would never have guessed that he had endured multiple major surgeries in his life. He was such a gentle, fun-loving, young teenager. Johnny was also a diehard Red Sox supporter. He would sit with his good friend Damon in a residential room and listen to all the games he possibly could, with the help of his hearing aid. His rooms at home and at the school were covered in Red Sox memorabilia.

One day, I called Johnny up for his traditional rendition of 'Take me out to the Ball Game,' which he liked to perform during a weekly sing-a-long in the school gym. I noticed that Johnny wasn't really feeling his usual cheery self, but he still wanted to sing his favorite team song. When he finished I yelled, "Give it up for Johnny! Great job buddy!" Everyone cheered. When the sing-a-long was over I asked him if he was doing okay. "Yeah," he replied, even though he looked a little tired. As always, Johnny was never one to complain about anything.

I went home that night like any other work night – tired and contemplating the day's experiences.

The next morning, my doorbell rang. I had the day off and I wasn't expecting visitors, so when I opened the front door I was surprised to be greeted by my workmates. "What's up?" I inquired, noticing how somber they all looked. Then, as tears began to flow down their cheeks, they broke the news.

"Johnny died this morning."

I couldn't speak. My work friends began to hug me one by one as I fought back the tears. "I'll be there shortly," I said.

When I arrived at the school I saw a police officer sitting by Johnny's bedroom door. My co-worker, Derek, and I were told that we could go in see him. As we stood by Johnny's bedside, I struggled to accept that just fifteen hours previously he was singing 'Take me out to the Ball Game' with all his school friends. I stood in shock. Later that day the school president addressed all of the department's staff. I couldn't hold back my own tears. Johnny had only attended the school for the blind for one year but had touched the hearts of so many people in that short time. In less than two weeks he had been scheduled to throw the first pitch at the Red Sox game. He had recently toured Fenway Park with his class, and just a few years ago got to meet the team as a wish granted through the High Hopes Foundation.

Johnny's family was so wonderful and supportive to him all his life. This was a great reminder of how precious my own family was to me. In fact, there were many times when I struggled with the reality of being so far away from them. I missed them, but I knew in my heart that I had to hold firm to the belief that I had my own path in life just as they had theirs. Through my healing work with the Family of Light I could accept that I was in the right place at the right time and with the right people. I could feel their protective guidance around me like an invisible cloak of Light and love. I began to experience this love as a palpable vibration in my day-to-day life. What I mean by this is that irrespective of what else was happening in my life, I could feel a sweet energy radiating from my heart center. The experience was exquisite. This was satisfaction; this was fulfillment; this was love without condition. And it seemed that all I needed do to sustain this divine experience was to give my attention to it. I found that to protect — and continue to protect — this experience of inner love became the most pressing and immediate goal of my life.

According to the Family of Light this love that I was experiencing existed in all beings on this planet. What was unusual is that now, because of the preparatory work I had done with the Family of Light, I was choosing to make this universal, unconditional love my primary reality. I was consciously doing whatever I could to experience this divine reality fully and continuously. To support me in this endeavor, in one of our sessions the Family of Light gave me some practical guidance:

"We greet you in the Light! We want you to know how beautiful and precious you are, how loved you are. You might say that increasing love on the Earth plane is the one plan, the plan of love and Light, which is unfolding in the universe in the perfect way. We are here to assist you in your ability to increase love in your dimension and to increase love in your own experience of life, in your own heart, body, mind, and spirit. It is this love that sustains you as you pass through all the lessons of life, as you pass through the many karmic experiences that are completing and dissolving. It is love that sustains you so that you create more and more love and do not create additional karma. It is love that is the Light that is who you really are, and it is love

that heals you. This feeling of love is the warmth that you describe. The vibration of love is very warm and very pure. There are varied frequencies and vibrations of Light and love, and higher love is being born into the Earth plane. Sustaining this vibration is the task at hand, and allowing your body to adjust to this vibration is your task at hand. As you open to spiritual guidance, we are healing the layers of your aura in alignment with your own soul. You have done great work around the heart chakra, (heart energy center) especially the inner perimeters in the emotional body, and this evening we will be working with your heart chakra at a deeper level. This might be seen as moving from the petals of a flower to the center of the flower. You may picture this flower on your chest and the center of the flower is where we are directing our healing forces, healing energies, during this session.

When you state that you would like to feel more warmth, understand that you will be feeling more energy in general. You will be more sensitive to energy and to the various vibrations that are around you, including love, joy, and peace. Also you will become more sensitive to the denser vibrations and, as you were saying, you will be finding ways to work with these energies so that you can be peaceful and at ease.

It is very important for you to connect deeply with others at the heart level. It is easier for you at this time to connect mentally and spiritually with others. There is some blockage at the level of the heart and the deep emotions in the second and third chakras. You are currently focusing a lot of your healing here, in the second, third, and fourth chakras, so that you can feel a deeper connection with others. There is old trauma, a wounded-ness, in these chakras and, therefore, a certain amount of shutting down or a lack of connection. This is why you experience wanting to connect and feel more. These areas are being healed even as we speak to you, and when you have concern regarding your purpose as a spiritual one — a spiritual teacher, a healer, a Light Worker — which you are, it is the wounded-ness in these chakras that comes up as a concern for you.

Trust that this healing is underway and that in time you will find you are connecting deeply, deeply, in the heart. Your concern around expressing spiritual ideas will go. We are bringing through higher frequencies of healing energy to uplift you and heal you. Use your mind, your will, and your heart to tune into these energies, tune into the guides around you, and to emulate the vibration of the Light Beings."

Even more compelling for me than the eloquence of their words, was the profound feeling of peace that always accompanied them. As I pictured the beautiful image of the flower in my chest, I was reassured that my old traumas, and my "wounded-ness" were being healed. In this session, and indeed in all my sessions, the Family of Light transmitted higher frequencies of healing energy which uplifted and supported me in emulating their vibrations. I would receive various tools and visualizations for learning to hold these higher vibrational energies in my consciousness or awareness.

During one session, a Light Being named Zargon explained the importance of inviting the higher energies and higher guidance into our lives.

"I am Zargon, and I am just to the left of Leslie. We [the Light Beings] are surrounding you, and I am telling you where we are to help you to sense and feel the vibration of the refined energy of your guides. Quacate is to your left, perhaps a foot from your body. Quacate shows his body in the form it was in the life where you knew him and that body sits in a bubble of Light. He shows you a translucent Light body. You are becoming ready to channel Quacate and bring his energy closer into your own aura. So, spend a few moments now consciously connecting with Quacate and inviting him to come even closer. It is always a matter of your inviting and allowing the energy of your guide to expand and merge with your own energy. The act of channeling the messages of the Light Beings gives you a tool to guide your life. It reminds you of your greatness, your expansiveness, and the energy that comes through you heals your life. You learn and grow and serve others in learning and growing. That is why you are opening to be able to channel. In truth, there is a great opening to channel all over the Earth plane, and as the new consciousness is birthed, channeling will become commonplace. In fact, the energy being channeled will be so present on this plane that "channeling" will be very different from what you now understand it to be. At this time you are bringing through messages of Light and thereby preparing yourself and others for this shift in consciousness."

In another session, I asked the Family of Light for more advice on the subject matter of holding the Light vibrations:

"We are interested in helping you with your question, "how do I hold the Light?" Well, first of all, you are already holding the Light, so we

approach this question with the desire, the intention, of supporting you in expanding that ability and becoming stronger and stronger in it. This would mean that your day-to-day state of being would be an elevated state as compared to where it is now. The process will involve healing and purification. This healing and purification can come about in an elevated way through your focus on the higher energies and on utilizing these higher energies. These energies are available to you on the Earth plane and can be of great help to you in fulfilling your desire to go higher, to be of service, to be abundant and happy. In fact it is these energies that bring about the increased liveliness and vitality that everyone on the Earth plane seeks. So it is important for you to learn how to draw this energy and model it. The many, many ways of healing that are becoming available on Earth all seek this end, this higher state of consciousness. What we offer to you now is a group of beings who teach about this energy, this Light, and who hold it at a certain level so that, with our support, you can go right to the Light and learn how to hold this Light for yourself — so that you can simply go to that higher state of being. This is an awakening of the refined energetic state that is part of who you are. You are alluding to your inherent union with the Light when you talk about being part of the higher consciousness that all is one. What we're saying is that this is a dimension of yourself that you can identify with at will and, by doing so you will uplift every aspect of your energy. You are multi-dimensional; you contain many levels, and all of these levels seek to go higher. Why not tune into the highest level and live from there? It is immediately healing to tune into these energies, and it is vitally important for you to become strong in this. Channeling, bringing through spiritual energy, is a very good way to practice tuning in, as channeling brings you into direct contact with this higher self that we speak of. So in one sense, what you are doing is becoming who you already are. Our goal is to assist you in this. You can work on yourself, but you also need help to know when you are not to work, when you are to let yourself be, to float, and to flow. There is a time for work, and there is a time for resting and play. This is all the truth. Eventually, as you begin to exist in a higher state more of the time, each of these activities becomes more and more Light-filled ... So, when you are experiencing channeling, in the presence of the Light Beings, you will often notice an increased state of well-being during and after the session. This state of well-being is what we are after. The question for you is how to tune into this state on your own, and how to do that at will and in a conscious structured way."

And so, the task at hand continued to be to become more and more accustomed to holding the Light. I had much more work to do to maintain and increase this awareness, but I was secure in the knowledge that I was in good hands.

Chapter 7

The Inner Healer

In my sessions with Leslie, the Family of Light would often work with my chakras, the energy centers in the subtle body. Within me these centers were, to a certain degree, blocked. The Family of Light told me that in the course of this lifetime, my chakras would be opened and brought into balance, the energy flowing through the centers and also working in them all to the same degree. They explained that this was important work, because as the chakras opened, I would gain better understanding of the process of deep inner healing I was undergoing, and the healing itself would be enhanced.

Through my research I understood that much had been written about the chakras, and how they're described differently depending on each writer's tradition, perspective, or experience. There were, however, certain aspects of the chakras on which everyone seemed to agree. The chakras were in the subtle body, which is the energy body that inhabits the gross physical form we usually call "the body." Each chakra had a particular location in the subtle body, and this was identified by a part of the physical body that the chakra was near. Each chakra was also associated with certain qualities and abilities as well as certain colors, sounds, and, according to many, even deities.

In one of my channeling sessions, the Family of Light surprised me by linking an upcoming medical procedure, surgery to correct a hernia, with the work of clearing my chakras. Here is what they said:

"Your hernia operation represents the mending of relationships and the mending of your way of connecting with others on the earthly as well as the spiritual planes. The second chakra and the connections you build out of this center have to do with deep emotional resonances and with womb-like love. There is a center of love and a center of the heart in the second chakra, and the healing of your hernia represents the healing of a wound in the heart of the second chakra that you have been carrying at the psychic level for many incarnations. The opportunity that has come in this life to heal this problem in the physical realm will also heal it in the emotional, mental, and the spiritual realms. It is important for you to incorporate understanding, Light, insight, growth, and healing on all of those levels at the same time you are attending to the physical level. So the body assists you in your psychic healing and is also a great teacher for you.

There is a sense of grief and broken-heartedness in this second chakra that you have been working with over time. Now you have an opportunity to release these energies and allow this part of your life to be healed. You'll be healing a wound, letting go of a scar. In terms of your karma, it is the time for you to deal with this. Although we could refer to specific relationships, and specific incarnations, which might be useful to you at some point, it is more important for you to understand that relationships in general will be healed. In other words, if we were to take a higher perspective and look at all your lives as one life, we would say that there is a place of disintegration that is about to be harmonized and brought into the whole, that will be integrated with the Light. If we were to speak about this in terms of evolution and growth, we would say it is a movement by which your individual relationships will be united with all of nature and all of life ... You're going to feel very deeply connected and safe in a way that you have not before felt. Some of the fear, the feeling of being unsafe, is unconscious for you. The operation is an opportunity for you to release that fear, the fear of relating and connecting and of being hurt because of it. If you take this higher perspective of this current aspect of your journey, you will be able to trust that spirit is with you."

What was most interesting for me regarding this reading was the way it played out in my life afterwards. After the operation, I found myself relating to my family and friends from a new space of self-confidence. I was able to express love more easily. Also shortly after the operation, I gained more and more confidence in my job. Eventually I was promoted into a supervisory position. My new-found sense of ease allowed me to assume a leadership role, taking an overview, giving directions, hearing complaints and criticism, and keeping my own center and my own sense of well-being in the face of it all. This was not a role I'd ever had before and, I think, not a role I ever could have held before. Now, it felt natural to me.

It was also through working with the Family of Light that I was able to understand why a leadership position would feel natural for me, as they told me I had held various leadership roles in past lives.

At another session, the Family of Light mentioned a particular lifetime when, while serving as a priestess, I was wounded and I shut down my psychic abilities in order to deal with the pain. This was how they described that particular lifetime:

"Quacate has been your teacher and your healer many times. As a student he instructed you in the ways of healing and spiritual practice in this lifetime we're going to look at now. At that time you developed your healing faculties beyond what you currently experience. When you are ready, in this life you will be reopening and reawakening these intuitive and psychic abilities. This includes telepathic communication with the spiritual realms.

The lifetime that comes forward through the memory bank for expression now is one you spent in a priestess school, a temple, where Quacate was a teacher and you were a student priestess. In this school certain children were received and trained in the ways of priestesses: healing, ritual, magic, meditation, intuition, and all forms of healing. This is a lifetime in which you developed a lot of psychic power and in which you worshiped the goddess and served many people as a healer and priestess. You were aware of the, shall we say, witch hunts, which started to happen with the Roman Catholic Church. This movement of the church annihilated the priestesses, who were raped and killed, many by burning or hanging. This is part of the reason you shut down your psychic abilities: stored in your memory banks of being psychically open is a lot of pain and trauma.

So, in this lifetime you have chosen to be in the body of man and to be one of the healers of gender imbalance. As you reopen your psychic and intuitive abilities, you will be releasing karma, letting go of the fear and pain you hold around those memories of what happened to you and to those you loved.

You are embodied now, as you were then, to help with the evolution of the human race, the completion of karma, and the fulfillment of the divine plan on Earth."

This session was quite a revelation. There were indeed many times in my present life when I would reflect on experiences of "shutting down" emotionally. Maybe some of these feelings were related to that "psychic shutdown" due to a soul memory of being raped and killed during the witch hunts. As I thought about this I was reminded of Ruth Montgomery's explanation that we were all living out our karma in this world while also living under the influence of our subconscious minds, unaware that an experience or tendency from a past life, either good or bad, was affecting our present actions, decisions, and behaviors. Still, I knew that my karma in this lifetime had its purpose and ultimately the path of the heart was about inner healing, service, and awakening to my divine reality.

During another session with Leslie, the Family of Light performed a chakra healing on me. They were joined in this session by Shaymar, whom I had apparently known in a lifetime in ancient Egypt. Here was the information I was given that day on the lifetime we had both shared:

"Each time you meditate and have energy work done, you are releasing much karma. Shaymar is present as part of the group of beings here connecting with your dimension. He is making his presence felt from another frequency, a phenomenon that can happen as the worlds become closer in frequency. Shaymar remembers your dropping of the body in that life, and he remembers helping with your burial. He also remembers the rituals by which you were assisted into the next life. He has just repeated the prayers of passage, with very beautiful chanting. In that life, Shaymar was a priest as were you. So, Shaymar, having finished Earth life, has come here to guide you once again.

He advises that you to stay open to guidance and says that you will know when to express yourself. He says you will know that everything you do is an expression of Light. He and all your guides are working to assist you in completing your Earth life at this time.

You have lived many lives, and in the past you have known many rituals. It is fine to utilize a combination of those that you remember and hold dear. That is good. That is a sign of consciousness rising on Earth, when souls remember many lifetimes and many prayers and many ways of knowing God. Remember the goal is Self-realization, completion of your karma. You are doing very well in regard to these and in regard to not creating new negative karma in this life. In fact you are feeling that inner struggle, as you are releasing karma from past lives and this current life. You are not creating new karma, and when you do, it is minimal and will be cleared almost instantly. That is true. You are doing much better than you realize. It is difficult for us to express this to you. You have moments when you experience peace about your journey and then there are many other moments when you, very humanly, experience doubt. Embrace your humanity. You are progressing nonetheless. Simply accept the best you can do. That is very good; it is serving you well. Truly, there is another world that you will pass into next — a world of beauty and harmony that you are discovering now inside yourself. In this other world, the weights and pressures of Earth's gravity and dense energies are no longer present; the experience of love and transcendence are the reality here. So, make the most of your sojourn on Earth and join us here soon. Blessings in the Light!"

Feeling a deep sense of gratitude to Shaymar and the Family of Light, once again I replied, in a whisper,

"Thank you! I love you!"

Chapter 8

Ask and You Will Receive

As the Family of Light continued to bring clarity to my healing process, I gained greater confidence in reaching the goal of that process. I began to feel that I could achieve full radiance and live from that place of equanimity and love in this very lifetime. Furthermore, I saw that the doorway the Family of Light were opening for me was open for all of humanity, and that it was our mission to assist each other in stepping through it into a new life. They told me that it was possible for each one of us to seek inner truth and to make the necessary shifts in consciousness required to live as fully-awakened human beings. All we had to do was ask, and with faith in the healing process we would receive everything we needed.

Later, the Family of Light also spoke of this exalted human potential and of their role in expanding human consciousness:

"You are made of Light. You are born of Light. You are receptors of Light. You are transmitters of Light. This is woven together in a complex dynamic system you call your "self." The healing angels are master technicians of your system of Light and they're here to guide you on your journey. We invite you to continue to meet with us and hear our guidance and messages and work with us on your energy field and body. This would be a very good way for you to meditate each day. We are guiding you every step of the way along a pathway that is very simple. It is our one essential message, that you are Light and that you are growing into a new space, a new dimension of Light and energy where it is required that you go through transformation so that you can adjust to this frequency of Light. We have been supporting you in your containment of Light. That is the essential work right now. This is the essential way to speak about it, although, of course, its ramifications are great and many.

There is a great potential for a subtle form of healing that would help each and every one of the beings on Earth, and yet the application of this healing is very new. You are a pioneer of this evolution. There are many pioneers in the Family of Light working on Earth at this time and we, together in the Family of Light, are working to guide you all into subtler and subtler forms of healing. And so, in the movement of Light on Earth, there is the continual emergence of new ground. Things are going quite well. It is a journey and a process to which you are highly tuned-in and which will benefit you and all those around you. Simply put, we are assisting you in achieving full radiance so that even in your earthly body, you will become a radiant Light Being of only a slightly different vibration and frequency than we angels. Our mission is a mission of love: to bring this message of love to all. It is true that there is no set way to experience this movement of Light ... You must stay tuned in to your heart and to what feels right to you in every moment ... This requires that you be adaptable. This requires that as you go through many speedy changes as you tune in, and tune in, and tune in to your own Self, as you experience what is right, now in this moment, and what is right in the next. As you are healed, you are becoming more and more sensitive, more and more Light-filled, and the changes in you are very rapid. What is appropriate one day may not be appropriate the next. Certain routines and practices that are woven into your existence are very powerful, but there is no one way to achieve greater radiance. It happens many different ways."

The Family of Light spoke a little more regarding my chakra healing, in particular the fifth and sixth chakras. The fifth chakra energy center is in the area around the throat, the center of communication and speech. The sixth chakra is known as the "third eye center" and is located between the eyebrows. The third eye is the spiritual center of psychic power, of visions and higher intuition. It is through the third eye that people can communicate telepathically and have visions of past lives and of the future. The Family of Light explained:

"You have had a slight malfunction in what we'll call the "computer chip" of your communication center. The throat chakra and third eye chakra have now evolved and have been progressively altered by us in your healing. What you have gained from this work is clarity. The healing of these two chakras has enabled you to become clearer in

formulating and articulating ideas. A lot of confusion has cleared up for you, and you are now remembering what you know ... This clarity is in every cell, in the wisdom of your very soul. The cloud of confusion that was created by repressed energies is clearing rapidly so that you can now remember basic truths and feel certain of them while maintaining a necessary flexibility about what truth is. We are speaking here of relative principles, and so we would call this "wisdom memory.""

During all of my sessions with Leslie I would sit on a chair or lie on a massage table while allowing the Family of Light to work with my energy through Leslie. I had made a conscious choice to allow them to remove anything that was blocking me from receiving divine love and guidance in my life. Even though I knew I was receiving much guidance and was grateful for it, I also knew that spiritual growth was not always easy. Letting go of my ego and the influence it had had over me was not going to happen overnight. I saw that I needed to have discipline to recognize those times when my ego was trying to trick me into identifying with life's dramas and rob me of the simplicity of experiencing the joy of the present moment. For instance, there were those moments when the voice of jealousy, envy, or unworthiness would whisper in my mind, distracting me from my true self. When I identified with these negative thoughts I found that I was cheated out of what could have been positive life experiences. In identifying with these negative thoughts, I would experience going through what the Family of Light once referred to as "the dark night of the soul." At these times, for example, the experience of rejection brought painful feelings of unworthiness, inadequacy, anger, jealousy, and loneliness to the surface of my consciousness. At times I would try to distract myself from experiencing these feelings by drinking alcohol to numb the feeling of not being good enough. In truth, I was worthy of love, as we all are, but I was blinded at times by an old karma that prevented me from receiving love because I didn't think I deserved it. With regards to relationships with women I would walk away from some beautiful, loving relationships as I didn't know how to fully embrace their love and instead look for acceptance in relationships that weren't available to me. This pattern would cause unnecessary pain for me and those I genuinely had much love and respect for. I forgot all the precious guidance I had received from the Family of Light and the great spiritual teachers who watched over me. Ultimately, I learned from the Family of Light that this sort of distraction, even the experience of the dark night of the soul, was simply part of being human; everyone makes mistakes. What mattered most was that we learned as we went along, that we gained in our wisdom.

I found that spiritual practice was crucial in helping me to stay in touch with my heart and to trust the process of healing I was undergoing. Without the discipline of my practices, I would continue to experience unnecessary suffering and pain — I would be, in other words, at the mercy of my ego. It was meditation, chanting, and spiritual study that gave me the perspective to be able to witness the negative voice of the ego and, in difficult times when I succumbed to it, to forgive myself, pick myself up, and move on. I could see that my mistakes were a means to learning, to growing, and to letting go of karma.

In one particular session with the Family of Light, I experienced an enormous amount of compassion concerning the dark corners of my mind, my "shadow self," as it was also termed:

"Do not be afraid of the dark corners or the closets of the rooms that hold darkness. This darkness is to be embraced. It is part of who you are, and you are to bring the Light there. Eventually, you will evolve into another state of being, which is no longer human but angelic, spirit, and so on, up through the gradations of spiritual beings and the various planes of existence with which you commingle on your spiritual journey. So let us say that you are doing some scrubbing in the heart chakra and that on Sunday, when you experienced the sadness, that was a cleanse. You are cleansing any so-called negative programming. You are cleansing any negative thoughts, including fear, mistrust, and doubt, that are not in alignment with love for yourself and, thus, love for others. As you achieve perfection, you are perfect each step of the way. Paradoxically and mysteriously, as with so many aspects of earthly life, each doubt and fear actually helps you to further your journey. This is why it appears. It can be a little hard to understand, and yet you do understand.

You are being deluged with golden and pink light in the chest and lung area by two angelic healers who are right now holding your chest ... Also your first two chakras are having trouble with their rotation, with spinning and taking in energy appropriately from the Earth plane. The guides are helping these chakras to get the spin happening clockwise so that the energy flows in a proper way for you in that area and so you can take in energy at the root and second chakra. There has been an imbalance, an expelling of energy, a loss of energy, and you have sometimes felt lost in terms of where and who you are on Earth, even though at the same time, spiritually, you do feel found. There has been a lack of grounding for you to this Earth plane. What will start happening now is that you will be increasingly more grounded to your work, your body, and your life here. You will feel more solid, more connected to your family and to all of human life. You will be connecting not in the old ways but in new ways. You will be connecting with other people in meaningful ways ...

The Light Beings are tending to the new young souls that are incarnating. In many cases they are incarnating with full knowledge of the spiritual world. They are incarnating with an awareness of multi-dimensional being-ness. You are at the forefront of that, as you know, holding that Light for others, like a beacon or lighthouse, guiding the way. Even as you go into your own dark closets, this is true. Also, as you know, there are those holding out their Light to you, guiding your way. The Light-force is very strong on this planet. Even though there are also, shall we say, forces of darkness, the Light is stronger, the love is stronger, and things are going quite well due to many open hearts and willing souls, willing to do their own work to support one another in the Light.

We are going to let Leslie use her hands now. We will work through her now. For you humans, there is nothing like the human touch."

Ah, I smiled as I agreed; there is nothing like the human touch for us humans. I was reminded once again of the immense compassion of the Family of Light and that if I wanted their help I only needed to ask for it, as their grace and my self-effort went hand in hand.

Also, their guidance could come in many different forms: through a book, a film, another person, or even through my own intuition. Any doubt or fear, any strong preconception could be an obstacle to my "hearing" their guidance.

I asked the Family of Light how we could all be supported in our communications with the higher realms. They responded:

"We want to continue to strengthen your ability to work with us, for the power between us for healing potential is very, very great. Many of the so-called miracle healings occurring on Earth are the result of cooperation with healing angels, and it is also true that when you humans block our help, however unconsciously, there is little that we can do. We can assist you in opening up, but it is always your choice. We are always here helping and supporting you, but it is your openness that turns the key. That openness, as you know, often requires a lot of prior healing around fear. And so each soul, each being, has its own plan for awakening and remembering and utilization of the angel realm, of the Light ...

You humans can relax in your journey. Most of you have a tendency to over-strive, and to over-strive in the wrong areas. We would like to convey that you can rest and utilize less energy in different ways to achieve the same or better results. This is part of your learning process, too: learning how to gauge using energy and working with spiritual energy, how to gauge your own progress, your own evolution."

One way I was able to remove energy blocks and old tendencies, I discovered, was to participate in spiritual retreats. The Family of

Light commented briefly on a retreat I was planning to participate in and on how my soul planned for me to find a yogic path:

"This summer while you are on retreat, you will be clearing a lot of karma in a very powerful way. You will be getting a lot of work done, and this plan of action was put in place by your soul a long time ago. Your soul whispered to you not only to come to America but to seek out the teachers of Light whom your soul was aware of and knew it would be important for you to link with. And so you've come to fulfill the plan of your soul. At the retreat you will be busy working on the mundane level as well as the spiritual level, and you will receive many, many great blessings from this experience."

The Family of Light reassured me that I had plenty of time to complete my karmic healing and awakening in this life and that this was a lifetime project I had undertaken. In one session they clarified for me both the nature of my ego and the way I could become free from its influence. A lot of this work involved continued healing of the chakras, particularly the heart chakra. They also spoke about my relationship with the seventh chakra. This chakra is sometimes referred to as the "crown center" and is associated with the crown of the head. When this center is fully open, a person experiences self-realization, meaning that their consciousness merges with the divine, with God. They said:

"There is still more to be cleared from the heart center. The heart center is a place where you will be doing a lot of work in this life. It is quite a focus for you. There is no hurry as it is a lifetime project, one

that you will go back to and enjoy time and again. There could easily be other chakras involved, and, indeed, there are other chakras involved in your life's plan. For example, the crown chakra and third eye are featured quite prominently in the lesson plan for you in this life. The third eye is important as you find your way in communicating and teaching. You are gaining in confidence, as well as humility. Your ego will begin to drop away from your communication, whether it's been the ego that's been holding you back or the ego that's been pushing you forward. You will achieve more balance in this area of communication as you gain experience.

The extremes of unbalanced communication would be, for example, "Who, me? I don't know much of anything," to the opposite pull of "I'm the one who knows." Coming to the center, in a balanced place, would be "This is what I can share," with an openness and humility, and "This is what I know, this is my truth." So that is happening.

You've had a big breakthrough in this past year in being able to speak with less fear. The energy work you've done cleared a lot of fear in many ways. That is one of the ways we can show you your transformation. It is important for you to take stock and see what you've learned and how you've grown because these are the experiences you will hold, and perhaps share. Your awareness of holding these experiences will create the space for others to have their own transformational healing, supported by you."

I expressed my gratitude to the Family of Light for the information, guidance, and healing I continued to receive from them. It was clear from them that even as I participated in my own personal healing and service, part of my life's role was also to support healing and transformation in others. I felt very excited about the future and the opportunities that awaited me. I took great comfort in their reassuring words:

"No matter what you do, it is all perfect."

Chapter 9

Atlantis and Ancient Egypt

From time to time I would request more information on the history of my soul from the Family of Light. When they revealed that my soul had lived in legendary Atlantis, I decided to do some research on this great civilization and its karmic connection to today's world.

Atlantis was thought to have disappeared in a day some twelve thousand years ago when the entire continent sank into the Atlantic Ocean, so I figured that the only accurate information I'd be able to get about this lost land was through a respected medium. Embarking on my research, I discovered the website of the internationally-active channeler known as Diandra, who headed an organization known as Inward Journey. Diandra channeled highly-evolved master souls from the spiritual realms, including a being named Salem, who was well-versed in the history of Atlantis and Ancient Egypt. According to Salem, these ancient worlds shared some striking similarities with our present era. It seemed there was much more to our history than we, as a collective human family, had realized. Salem explained that the experience of Atlantis and ancient Egypt was real for many of us who are alive today simply because we were also incarnated at that time. He said that because we were present then, we now carry the memory of those ancient times in our personal and collective subconscious. What was most significant about this, says Salem, is that during the time of Atlantis, ancient Egypt, and another lost land named Lemuria, humankind reached stupendous heights of understanding. This meant that the great teachings and stories of this ancient time, an earlier Golden Age, were a part of us now, even as we entered this new, current age of awakening and enlightenment.

According to Salem, the civilization of Atlantis had its origin in a tiny population of souls that came to our planet for the purpose of helping humanity. This cadre of advanced souls came from another galaxy to awaken humanity's dormant spirituality and to give instruction on life's inherent beauty and ultimate purpose. Before these beings came, humanity was struggling to survive. Warring tribes engaged in a continuous round of battle; there was no overview, and no real guidance or leadership. The strongest ruled, but only for a day, then another round of fighting would begin, and another victor would emerge. Individuals in this beleaguered world would pray, asking questions in their hearts about the existence of God and asking, if such a divine being did exist, that He send them some relief. In answer to these prayers, beings traveled from another galaxy and set up a community to teach humanity of their own beauty, power, and love. This was Atlantis.

The Diandra messages, I realized, were yet another source of information bringing to the surface of human awareness the subject matter of UFOs and intelligent beings living beyond our own planet. Salem confirmed that civilizations most people today generally believed to be mythological were indeed real.

He continued by saying that Atlantis began as a tiny community populated by beings from another galaxy. Once they had set up some buildings and infrastructure, these intergalactic visitors went out into the countryside, meeting one tribe after another, telling people about the purpose of their new community, and inviting them to join it if they chose. The basic message to human beings was that in this community they could find a higher purpose for their lives. Survival would not be an issue, for in Atlantis they would have food and housing to meet their needs, and so much more: art, philosophy, and science. Some human beings chose to move to Atlantis, and once they had entered this heavenly realm they seldom wished to go back home, said Salem.

In time Atlantis grew, and the human population began to reawaken to its own divine potential. At the time Atlantis began humanity had descended to an extremely low level of understanding. People were in awe as they entered into this new, and for them, God-like community. They began to live in a way that reflected their own highest capacities and, as this happened, the beings who had come to teach began to withdraw. These teachers would return to Atlantis from time to time to check on the progress of their students, but they ceased to play a role in the operation of this new civilization and in the instruction of humankind. Even though many of us alive today were a part of the population of Atlantis, we have effectively forgotten the extraordinary beings that came to Earth and set up the structure to help us regain the consciousness that we had lost.

There were many temples in Atlantis, explained Salem, and one of the most significant was the great Temple of Healing. Earth became known throughout the solar system for the power of this Temple of Healing, and countless beings made intergalactic journeys to consult with the healers there. It was partly for this reason that Earth became the place in the galaxy where souls from widely-divergent worlds could meet and intermingle and gain greater understanding, not just of medicine and the healing arts but also of one another. The Temple of Healing opened a possibility for intercultural understanding that had never existed before. There was also the Temple of Philosophy, which provided a new kind of forum for discussions about life — the nature of life, the purpose of life, the divergent forms life takes, the very creation of life. Atlanteans were extremely intelligent and they loved to probe and explore, to contemplate and discuss. It was these very souls, deeply embedded in the philosophical traditions of Atlantis, that later incarnated as the Greek philosophers. In fact, said Salem, the first mention of Atlantis comes to us from Plato. The philosophers of Atlantis were continually advancing their understanding of life, and they extended their focus to include life throughout the galaxy. Their understanding of the solar system was much more advanced than ours is today.

So the question of intergalactic space travel was identified by Salem as an integral part of the lives of our ancient ancestors. While there were physical spacecraft, most of this intergalactic travel happened on the astral plane, through energy transference. Atlanteans were the masters of energy; they understood it as it has never been understood on this planet before or since. Once we truly understood energy, said Salem, there would be nothing that we would not be able to achieve in this world. The beings that founded Atlantis gave humanity enough knowledge about energy that the citizens of Atlantis were able to build an advanced world with relative speed and ease. And yet, as we well know from our experience on the planet today, science and technology are not sufficient unto themselves. In time, Salem says, the Atlanteans became consumed by their technology, and the imbalance eventually led to the downfall of their great civilization. The very technology that was initially used to better human life became the tool of its undoing. The technological advances they had brought to fuition began to be guarded by an intellectual elite, who then used these powers to serve their own interests. The resulting struggle for power was not unlike the internecine warfare that happened before the creation of Atlantis, only now the instruments of war were tremendously powerful. The leaders of Atlantis became intoxicated with their power to create, and what they created had such density that the landmass couldn't sustain the very weight of what was taking place. For years the Temple of Healing had not been in service, and visitors from elsewhere in the galaxy had ceased to come; now the Earth itself could no longer sustain Atlantis.

Salem explained that as Atlantis was falling, the leaders, the very people who were responsible for its destruction, sent out a plea for help. But at that point nothing could be done; Atlantis was almost void of spiritual Light and wisdom. Ultimately, there were only a few survivors, beings who were the least encased in their own fears, the purest in spirit.

Salem recounts many stories from this point in the history of Atlantis, and the one most interesting to me is, not surprisingly, the one that involves us today: one of the final masters of Atlantis promised that if human consciousness ever rose again to the level of the Atlanteans' consciousness at its height, then once again on the planet Earth we would know the beauty and peace of that earlier Golden Age. I was beginning to sense now that humanity had indeed reached that exalted point of scientific and technological evolution, and that this time we were being given sufficient space to understand our knowledge from a spiritual perspective.

During a session with Leslie, I was informed by the Family of Light that on a subconscious level humanity had already made a pledge to take this giant leap in consciousness and that it was just a matter of time before this consciousness shift, or paradigm shift, fully manifested on Earth. They said that this process was well underway and that humanity was now waking up from its spiritual amnesia. I was beginning to understand in a new light that what now seemed to be chaotic in the world was really just the destruction of an ego-based reality, steeped in greed and fear, and that a new dawn filled with love and understanding was on the horizon.

Salem continued by stating that it stands to reason that those of us who have a great interest in the stories of Atlantis were probably there. Over the years, there has been speculation about the possibility of Atlantis rising again. And yet according to Salem, Atlantis was not just a physical landmass; it was a state of consciousness, a point of awareness. Time itself was an illusion, and so, if we wished, we could relive the best of Atlantis today if we choose to. There are those of us who see it as our conscious goal to reconstruct the Golden Age of Atlantis — and to do it better, he said. We can do this by continuing to explore the divinity and beauty of our own humanity. Every time we meditate, every time we send love and thoughts of Light, every time we pray for a universal benefit, every time we love without condition, we are resurrecting Atlantis. We are bringing the consciousness we knew in the Golden Age of Atlantis into existence on today's Earth.

This prospect was tremendously exciting to me. By learning from our past, we could learn to avoid the grief and hardship of repeating our mistakes. By learning from our past, we could create a world where peace and tolerance are the mode of the day. By learning from our past, we could have the best of the ancient world and avoid its downfalls. We could have a Golden Age that doesn't disintegrate.

Salem also spoke at length about ancient Egypt, explaining that much of the knowledge of Atlantis found its way to Egypt many years later. As human consciousness began to rise in ancient Egypt, once again souls came from a distant world in another galaxy to engender in the people of Earth an awakening, an awareness of humanity's inner greatness. After a long period of dormancy, humanity began once again to feel the stirrings of creativity within the soul. Those who were awakened rose to positions of leadership and imposed controls on the rest of the population. The failures of Atlantis seemed to be embedded within humanity, and there was a fear that if the masses had the freedom of uncontrolled creativity, civilization would once again annihilate itself. The leaders of ancient Egypt felt that they could entrust no one but themselves with the power of knowledge. In time, however, others in this world were also awakened, and spiritual groups came into being throughout the general population of ancient Egypt. They quietly pursued knowledge in their own spheres, and because there was no disruption of the general order, the leaders allowed these spiritual groups to continue and to flourish. Salem said that it was these spiritual communities among the general population that built the pyramids, the wonders of ancient Egypt. The Egyptians did this by working with pure energy, pure vibration, to restructure and to move material forms — skills that they learned from the souls that had come from another world in another galaxy.

At the same time the pyramids were being created, the people of Egypt were also using their knowledge of energy to create all manner of art and to explore all forms of esoteric science. Much of what the Egyptians discovered in ancient times has become shrouded in mystery. Though the Egyptians began to remember the time of Atlantis and another civilization of old, Lemuria, they too fell prey to political power plays. Yet another mighty civilization was brought down by the thirst for power.

Salem concluded his discourse on these ancient lands by assuring that it was safe for us to step into our own reality and spirituality. He did, however, explain that we had a choice. Our planet was evolving rapidly and there would be those that are more familiar with their fear-based existence and may feel safer in their belief of the ego system they created. If that was their choice, then that was their right, he said. But it does not have to be the reality of all the population.

We all had the power within us to choose to live in a world that says that my reality is not that. My reality is love.

For me, it was no coincidence that so many messages from various sources carried the same import: that a momentous opportunity for spiritual transformation and a shift in human consciousness lay on humanity's doorstep. Also, I thought, when Salem was referring to intergalactic beings, maybe that included the Ashtar Command? The Ashtar Command had said before that more and more people would be coming into the awareness of their purpose in our skies and their millions of space craft. There were already so many people interested in UFOs now — many, in fact, who claimed to have information on, sightings, and even contacts with beings from other worlds. When Salem said that what was taking place was our evolution I believe he was pointing to humanity's ability to choose love and truth over greed and ego, thereby paving the way for us to embrace the higher celestial realities and raise humanity to even greater heights than those reached in the ancient times. We were co-creators in a cosmic process of enlightenment that would lead to a complete transformation of our planet.

Chapter 10

The Inner work

After sharing the messages of the Ashtar Command in Ireland and the United States in the early and mid-nineties, spending the following years focusing on my work in the school for the blind, and continuing my sessions with Leslie, I was often reminded by the Family of Light that the "inner work" I was doing would continue to be very important to my spiritual awakening. I found that one of my greatest challenges was to heal aspects of myself I hadn't before acknowledged. Leslie and my guides were assisting me in facing myself, in going deep into my soul and cleaning house, so to speak. This necessarily took time as there were many crevices and long-darkened corners within me that needed my awareness, attention, and acceptance. Part of the process of inner cleansing was to embrace these darker parts of myself – my "shadow self" – with love and compassion. Even though in previous lifetimes I had served humanity and gained spiritual understanding I also recognized through my work with Leslie that in other lifetimes I had served my own interests too. My guides didn't dwell on the subject of these self-serving lifetimes, but instead focused on the importance of my trusting this healing process so fully that I could accept whatever pain I was experiencing on my life path as a natural outcome of my own past actions and a benefit to my spiritual growth. So, as the Family of Light explained to me before, whenever feelings of loneliness, unworthiness, inadequacy, anger, or jealousy would arise in me, I had to remind myself that these were the dark corners of my mind that were being cleared out as a natural part of the healing process. I was told that with faith and self-effort I would be able to bring the light of knowledge into any challenging situation and that in this way I would be able to fully experience my emotions, let go, and move on. Understandably, many people on the spiritual path had trouble with the inner cleansing that comes with spiritual awakening. It can be extremely difficult for anyone to face himself or herself; it seems to be a natural human tendency to build a strong defense around the ego and shut down our awareness so that we can protect ourselves from feeling the pain of the past. Life will always have its challenges, and there are times when I didn't want to look closely at what those challenges were or how to cope with them. Part of any process of personal expansion involved my acknowledging the pain lodged within me. This was the pain of an accumulated memory referred to in yoga as "karmic impressions." I knew I had to experience this pain in order to release the impressions enabling me to move into a higher awareness of myself and the world.

This inner cleansing was an important part of the spiritual journey, but it was not, according to my guides, the whole journey.

The goal was to experience my inner divinity in every moment of life. My guides told me that when the right was right — when, as they put it, it was "ordained" — they would hold me in the Light as I released my old karmic patterns and the negative tendencies of my mind. They told me that I would later recognize these experiences as "breakthroughs" and that through them I would reach a new level of self-awareness. This is, in fact, how it was happening for me.

I was greatly supported in this process by my regular practice of meditation. In meditation I was able to get in touch with deeper levels of my being, levels of my soul that were beyond emotions and mental chatter. In this inner space I could recognize my negative emotions for what they were. Clearing these emotions would happen in various ways, through creative expression or simply through the cleansing release of tears. This point in the process would sometimes be filled with guilt and self-judgment, and yet my guides described it as most holy. They said that at these times, it was especially important for me not to give credence to the pain of my self-recrimination, to the feeling that something terrible was happening in my life, or that I had somehow gotten it all wrong, all of which I would sometimes do. None of this is real, they said. It is not who I am; it need not reflect the reality of my life. With the help of my guides and my own steady practice, I was able to recognize that the insecurities that arose were simply past impressions being dislodged from where they had been buried deep within my subconscious. These negative impressions had affected so much of my life that they had prevented me from living fully and experiencing the beautiful state of being that was natural to us all. In order to reach the goal I had to have faith in the timing of my own spiritual journey. So remembering my true self and true nature through spiritual practice was absolutely key to my having a smoother path back to full consciousness.

As part of my inner work my life was very often quite solitary. This solitude was good for me; it allowed me to focus on my healing process. I had the time, for instance, to reflect on my early years, on my upbringing in Belfast. I recalled how I sometimes struggled to conform to the cultural "strong man" image growing up where I would attempt to master the art of "keeping it all in" with regard to personal feelings. Still, with that being said, I had so much to be grateful for regarding my culture. I thought about my early twenties when I'd been a drummer in various cover bands in and around Belfast. I played in pubs around the university area and, in the north and west of the city; I played in clubs such as the Highfield, Glen Park Social, the Felons, St. Johns, and the Marty Forsythe. During these gigs, especially the charity events, again and again I would witness the generosity of my fellow countrymen and women. This was a generosity of spirit, an inherent kindness and friendliness, and I could see, in retrospect, how strongly I was influenced by these shining qualities. Being a part of the Irish collective was like living inside a huge and compassionate heart where love was expressed through actions more than words. I experienced the Irish people as preferring to "walk the talk" rather than to "talk the walk" in this all-important matter. There was always somebody who needed a helping hand, and there were always some in the community who would step up to the plate and give what they could. Even those people who were struggling financially would dig deep into their pockets and give. It was a beautiful expression of a maxim I once heard: "Out of oppression comes character."

My inner work reflections and contemplations also led me to remember moments in my life when I had been saved in some way or another by a higher power, as I believed.

When I was eighteen, I was crossing the Andersonstown Road in Belfast one evening when a car sped through a red light and hit me. The impact was so strong that I was flung into the air and thrown about fifteen yards from where the car had hit me. To my surprise, and to the amazement of those who had seen the collision, I got up off the street almost immediately, dusted myself off, and began to walk away as if nothing had happened. I noticed the car's dented hood and its occupants staring out through the shattered windscreen, so I reassured the shocked driver that I was okay. I then proceeded to walk into the local Chinese takeaway to order a curry. I remember the woman in the restaurant saying, "Is everything okay out there? Is the ambulance on its way? That sounded like a really bad accident." I told her, "Everything's okay. It was me that was hit, and I'm fine."

"I don't believe you," she said.

"No problem," I said, and I proceeded to order a chicken curry. A few minutes later she gave me my order and wished me a good night, but she still refused to believe that I'd been hit by the car. The friends I was with, who also had seen the accident, could hardly believe that I was hardly injured at all.

A few years earlier I had been in another accident with the same result: I was the passenger in a milk truck that skidded on the road and did a 180-degree turn before smashing into a taxi. Then, too, I could have been killed, but I walked away virtually uninjured. When I took the time to think about these two incidents I knew I was being protected by someone, somewhere, and that my life really did have a purpose.

While doing this inner work, I was being given the opportunity to see that everything that I had ever experienced from the day I was born — where I was raised, the people that surrounded me, every job I had held — was a part of my life plan, and that all of these experiences were designed to bring me to a more perfect awareness of who I truly am. The events of my life were my karma being played out. My decisions to leave my homeland for the United States and to meet the people who influenced me were all part of a soul plan that was written long ago. As part of my spiritual transformation, the Family of Light were helping me to see my destiny more clearly, to work through my challenges with honesty and integrity, and — most significantly — to be happy in my life. They were teaching me how to "hold the Light" as I continued through my challenges, reflections, and meditations.

During one particular session with Leslie the Family of Light offered me yet more insight into holding the Light:

"You can become stronger and have an even deeper experience of holding the Light at every moment in every day. This is what you are working toward. When you are in this state, your heart is open and you let go; you are compassionate and there are no troubles or fears. If a facet of you experiences any density, it is easily supported and resolved with the Light. Any energy can flow through you and not disturb this centered state of Light, and this is the state we want you to become increasingly accustomed to. In fact, it is you who have

requested our help in this. And so, here we are together in the Light. You are the Light of the world. You might also say that Jesus, being of Light, is our supervisor. We, being a team of Light workers in the Family of Light, include you. You are the star seeds who came to this planet to bring Light, and you are awakening to your purpose. It is time. You sometimes experience limitations but these limitations will soon be dissolved.

Think of yourself now as going even higher, and allowing this higher state, and allowing greater good for yourself, which then translates out to others. YOU MUST LOVE YOURSELF FIRST, for only in loving the self can you know how to love the other. Truly there is no separation. It does begin in your own heart. We are blessed by this interaction. Peace be with you. Blessings in the Light!"

Later, the Family of Light would inform me that I would soon have a spiritual teacher here on Earth. I got very excited over this prediction. As inspiring and supportive as it was to receive guidance from the spiritual realms, I knew that a physical teacher could also greatly support me in holding this centered state of Light and help me to stay focused on my path. As with almost everything else my guides had told me, this prediction did manifest.

One day I asked Leslie about hatha yoga, the ancient practice of postures and breath work that enhances a student's ability to sit for long periods of time in meditation. Leslie suggested that I try the yoga classes that were offered at a local ashram (a place for spiritual practice and retreat). Leslie explained that this ashram was connected to an Ancient Indian yoga tradition with a lineage that stretches back for thousands of years. She had a photograph of the living meditation master of this lineage on a little table in her meditation room. Leslie told me that this was her spiritual teacher.

I very much enjoyed the hatha yoga class and the atmosphere of the ashram. The people there were friendly and welcoming, and I felt immediately at home there. In addition to hatha yoga classes the ashram also offered sessions of meditation and chanting, and within a very short time I was drawn to attend these as well. Everything in the ashram seemed familiar to me, so when I returned to Leslie's house, we discussed my feelings about this. Leslie started picking up on one of my previous lifetimes in India, and then we invited the Family of Light to comment on this. They said that the lifetime Leslie was picking up on was one in which I had lived in an ashram in the Himalayas, the sacred mountains of North India, Pakistan, Tibet, and Nepal. In that environment I worked, studied, and grew spiritually under the guidance of a master yogi.

I felt very fortunate that in this lifetime I had once again made a connection with the spiritual traditions of India and a meditation master and teacher. I enjoyed the spiritual retreats and many visits to the ashram, and found my teacher to be a great source of strength for my inner work, guiding and reassuring me on my path.

Chapter 11

The Age of Aquarius

As my spiritual sojourn entered the new millennium I began travelling back to Belfast to see my family more frequently. Following three family weddings in eighteen months I realized how much I missed evryone so I began travelling back to Ireland again regularly. I accepted that I was not the spiritual renunciant of former lifetimes and that I was free to visit my family and friends in Ireland whenever I wished to do so.

During my visits home over the following years I noticed a great transformation in Belfast and the north of Ireland. Peace had come to Ireland, just as the Family of Light had predicted. I witnessed a graphic demonstration of this transformation in August 2007 when I attended the annual West Belfast Festival, Féile an Phobail. This week-long festival began in 1988, during some of darkest days of the Troubles as a way to boost morale and show the world that the people of West Belfast were a good, fun-loving, and caring community.

While on the tour of Milltown Cemetery — always a significant part of the festival — I met two policemen who were also taking part in the tour. One of them told me that his aunt was buried in this cemetery, and I shared with him that my mother and several of my family members were buried there also. When the tour arrived at the Republican plot that contained the grave of IRA volunteer Bobby Sands, the policeman and I were still chatting. Standing with a policeman at the edge of these IRA graves, I recognized the significant change that had come to Ireland; a few years before, the police would never have attended such an event. For them to be seen standing by the graves of IRA volunteers would have been unthinkable – unless they were supported and surrounded by the British Army. They wouldn't have been attending this event unless they were patrolling it, and they certainly wouldn't have considered showing respect at the graves of IRA volunteers. Furthermore, this was the very spot where I had witnessed Michael Stone try to kill Gerry Adams with grenades back in 1988.

When I returned to my dad's that day I felt immense gratitude to God and all those who had worked so hard to make this new Ireland a reality, including, unbeknown to most, the Family of Light and the Ashtar Command. There was still much work to be done but I took comfort in knowing that Ireland was changing for the greater good as part of a cosmic process, not just an Irish peace process. The stars had indeed moved.

In contemplating this astrological view, the realignment of the planets, I thought about an old 1960s musical, called *Hair*. One song in particular, the Fifth Dimension's 1969 hit "Aquarius" captured beautifully the spirit of these historic times, as they sang of peace and love, harmony and understanding, mystical revelation and personal liberation. According to one source, the Age of Aquarius that the song referred to would begin 2160 years from the birth of Christ. Rob Hand, Dane Rudyhar, and Sir Isaac Newton all put that point a hundred years earlier, at 2060. And according to Carl Jung, the shift has already taken place, having happened sometime between 1997 and 2000. What I found most interesting in all of this was not the precise timing of this evolutionary period, but the fact that so many disparate people have spoken of it, and that, according to most of them, the time is either really close or already upon us.

As part of this cosmic shift, humanity's remembrance of its soul origins, I remembered something I had read in the book *Seat of the Soul*, by Gary Zukav regarding humanity's spiritual identity. He claimed that our souls sit at the core of our being, a positive force that exists beyond time and space, and loves unconditionally. Our soul is multi-sensory; even as we inhabit our three-dimensional body, our soul can see beyond our present reality and experience into the fourth and fifth dimensions. It was able to make that step into higher dimensions based on personal evolution. This meant that two people walking down the same street at the same time could experience dramatically different realities: one might see a spirit guide or angel where the other sees only a three-dimensional reality.

I read of a related astronomical event that was considered a sign of the changing times involving the planet Venus. In June 2004, for the first time in 122 years, Venus would begin to cross between the

Earth and the Sun, creating the rarest of eclipses. This eclipse was referred to as the "Transit of Venus." Its significance to the dawning of a new age was explained in "The Miraculous Venus Transit," an article by Patricia Diane Cota-Robles that appeared in an electronic newsletter, LightNews.us. The article explained that when Venus passed between the Earth and the sun during this transit humanity would begin to experience an amazing transformation with all life evolving here. Many people, the article said, were referring to this cosmic moment as the starting point of the permanent Golden Age. When I first read this I was tremendously excited. What this writer predicted resonated with everything the Family of Light had been saying for years. The paradigm shift would be a grand cosmic event. However, I realized that this shift was not going to happen by itself. We were all co-creators in this cosmic process, and we all had a part to play.

Chapter 12

Starseeds

The Family of Light had spoken to me about the cosmic origins of humanity. I thought it would be a good idea to revisit a session which included revelations about our soul origins. Furthermore, by sharing more details on these cosmic origins with others, I felt that any public suspicion associated with UFOs due to Hollywood's fear-projected "alien" movies could be alleviated. My intention now was to help create the space for not only the politicians but the public to seriously consider the noble intentions of the Ashtar Command, and their benevolent nature.

In this particular session the Family of Light spoke of "starseed" souls. This referred to those "old souls" incarnated on Earth who hold within their soul memories experiences on planes of existence other than Earth. In the session they began by saying:

"Greetings in the Light. You are channeling radiance more than you know, and you are opening to channel continually as you connect more deeply with the higher dimensions. This process, as you experience it now from the Earth plane, is truly an adjustment. The very cells and molecules, therefore bones and structure of your system, are altering. Consider the Light Course [a recent group course facilitated by Leslie] *you have taken in your group to be a momentous movement forward into greater clarity, service, and understanding. We are teachers and healers and the bringers of the new dawn, the new consciousness, to this plane."*

They then responded to my request for more clarity on "starseeds." Their revelation, which included part of my own soul history, was pleasantly startling:

"You, Paul, came here from another dimension of reality and began to participate in the patterns here on this beautiful planet, seeking to bring your wisdom and your leadership to this plane. You have a commitment to see it through, and so you shall. More and more you are remembering what it is like to be in another dimension and to be the energy that you are, whether you are in the body or not in the body. As you remember more of who you are, your journey on the Earth plane becomes easier and simpler, more beautiful and more powerful. This awakening is happening all around the globe and is having quite an effect on the rest of the universe. We can say that everyone is excited by the growth of Light. There is more to come and a lot to do. There are many, many, many that need help and assistance in awakening. They will cross your path in many different

93

ways. So, although you carry divine intelligence and the culmination from all your evolvement of other existences, it is true that you are in an incubation period. This is not so much training as it is a matter of perfect timing and awakening for you. Were you to awaken suddenly, it could be too much for your world, your system, and could cause a breakdown. So you are pacing things according to your needs. This is the truth and it is perfect."

How many people, I thought, have been told that they've had experiences on other planes of existence as part of their soul evolvement? Not too many, I'm sure. Still, my mind remained opened to the Family of Light's revelation that many on Earth were awakening to this higher reality and historic shift in consciousness. The Family of Light continued:

There are many links between earthlings and the beings of other galaxies. We have mentioned this to you before. There will be a continued integration of beings. You did come very early on to supervise, to help set up life on Earth, and also to manage the early society that was here. You will remember more and more about that as is needed for your current purpose here on Earth, which is to bring Light, teach, and be a community leader. This will be a family of leaders and not the current type of leadership. This will be fraternity."

I was reminded at this point that Quacate was still an important guide for me. He was a transition guide who was helping me to open up in order to connect more deeply with him and communicate the messages of other guides. The Family of Light concluded this session with the following:

"Throughout the period of this Light Course, your awakening and remembering will increase. We are close, and here to help you in every way. Each time you have a session, an energy treatment, it is a conscious opening and invitation for us to adjust your energy for the changes you are going through. Everything is taken care of. We are glad you are conscious and connected to us, and can feel such good faith. We must say that the veil of illusion catches many. The mass beliefs in this reality can be quite challenging to separate from. As Jesus said, "Be in this world but not of it." This is what you are undertaking, and you will find that it becomes easier and easier. There will be more challenges and we will be with you. Yours in the Light, always. We bid you adieu."

This was quite a lot to digest. As exciting as this revelation was I wasn't sure what I was supposed to do with the information. I certainly wasn't inclined to immediately rush out and tell friends and family that the Family of Light said that we were multidimensional in our essence and that many of us were old souls with experiences from beyond the Earth's three-dimensional reality. Still, I was grateful to them for sharing this part of my soul history with me. In fact, I could hardly wait to speak with them again regarding "soul history" and starseeds.

I called Leslie requesting another session almost immediately and once again asked the Light Family for further insight, and once again their revelations were broad in scope.

"Good evening. Greetings. We are happy to speak with you. We are delighted that you wish this encounter of intelligence and that you request our information and knowledge which is really the same knowledge that dwells within your own soul. We consider ourselves to be a link, or conveyor, to help you connect with your own wisdom and knowing. You really have the power to answer any and all questions that arise within your being. Channeling is one of the ways that you answer your own questions by using the tool of the channel, and of channeling, to see and know your own truth ... We are very interested in your progress on your journey as this also influences and affects our dimension. Also, at times through this channel, there are specific ones — various teachers and masters — that come forward and speak from different dimensions."

The Family of Light then spoke of one particular plane of existence that my soul regarded as "home:"

"Everything is known to you within your soul. There are many worlds, dimensions, and realities besides the Earth plane. You carry within your memory bank experiences of other dimensions. The plane of existence from which you came is not spoken of or known in your life at this time. It is a place where the force fields are very different. What you know as gravity does not exist there, and yet, because of the make-up of the energy, there is not the opposite, or lack, of

gravity. There is neither. People are not floating around as in anti-gravity, or down on the Earth. It is a completely different structure. The life forms there include what you would on Earth call the animal realm and also beings with bodies similar to that of the humans of the Earth plane. It is a dimension of love and peace. It is also a dimension on which many of the myths and archetypes that you deal with here on the Earth plane are nonexistent. It's a different kind of story that is happening there. In fact, it is not a drama story with a motion to achieve something. On that plane there is a lot more of simply being. It is also a place where there is a lot of healing, as you would call it, and a growth of a different kind than what you experience here on the Earth plane. And yet we do experience great spiritual growth on the Earth plane. On that plane personal growth happens much more on an internal level — on the level of, shall we say, evolution to a natural state of being. On that plane you can also receive degrees according to what it is that you choose to study, or to achieve. However, there is not a hierarchy or competitive set-up. In that realm beings are exploring the application of love, Light, and creation in a very, we could say, subtle way. There is also interaction between beings on that plane with beings on other planes in the universe to formulate teams of cooperation and service and to facilitate the interchange of energies. In other words, there are beings that travel from that plane — in a mental way and also in a physical way — to other dimensions to experiment with creation. Or they travel to the Earth plane to support the evolutionary leap that is happening here.

Another aspect of that plane is most of the denser and darker energies are not present. There are what you would call disagreements or conflicts, but these are negotiated peacefully and harmoniously. So, part of your memory bank reminds you of living in this place, and even though you may experience longing for that place, know that this longing is a limited experience in the whole picture. Choices have been made to experience different planes of existence, and in fact, to travel and inhabit other planes in order to assist and serve those living there who need help. As well as the differences, there are many similarities to Earth. In fact, the Earth plane is becoming more similar to that plane. For example, the telepathic realm is opening up on Earth, and that is very much alive and a way of communicating on your home plane."

From time to time during my sessions I would experience an incredible feeling of love emanating from the Family of Light. At times tears of gratitude would flow down my cheeks. This particular session was one of those times. As they spoke I experienced a deep sense of gratitude for all they were doing in support of my personal journey and the healing of the entire planet. They concluded the session with these words:

"You have come here to learn to love and be happy in the constructs and confines of what you find in the force fields of this planet Earth and, at the same time, to assist others around you in this achievement. You are being assisted as well. Even though your guides have stated that there is an achievement, at the same time there is really nowhere to get to, as in simultaneous time the goal has already been achieved. You are experiencing this moment in time as part of a time frame, and yet the evolutionary leap has already taken place. All there is to do is

to BE. And in that BEING, there is a great joy and a powerful creative potential. So, we remind you to open to the possibilities given to you in this Earth plane. What happens here on the Earth plane affects even your home plane because it then elevates this game of life to a whole other level. It is like when a child in the family grows up and becomes part of the team, then the team can take on greater projects. So you live in a time construct, although time is simultaneous, and you are completing a project, although all there is to do is be. These are the seeming paradoxes of the universal life. As you evolve, the paradoxes can be held and contained by the consciousness so that your confusion melts away and you are set free. There are many great teachers and great paths to follow. Everyone is seeking this joy, this happiness, and the great teachers are all offering this experience of love. You also offer it to one another, and that is important to continue. Love is not always peaceful, and yet love is peace — again, a seeming paradox. See the example of the great teachers that you know that are not always peaceful on one level as they express themselves and that is important for you to contemplate. Your heart is full of Light, and you are in a timeframe process of unburdening your heart of the past. You can do that simultaneously with being in the present.

And so, be happy. Keep staying with that goal, and you will move into that space more and more. With peaceful blessings, we say, good night!"

As I traveled home after this session I remember observing the people on the street, on the bus, and on the subway with new eyes.

I smiled as I thought, "One day all of humanity will recognize its multidimensional origins and truly live in peace." Disclosure and acceptance of the universal brotherhood and sisterhood was inevitable. I promised the Family of Light that I would do my best in taking every opportunity to support the cosmic consciousness awakening of humanity and its impending paradigm shift.

Chapter 13

The Federation

In further exploring the reality of intergalactic life I revisited the Eternal Values discourses by Fredrick Von Mierers. In one of his lectures he explained that the Earth is like a school. Souls reincarnate again and again on the Earth school until they "graduate," meaning until they finish up their karma and experience union with God. Once they have transcended the Earth plane, they are free to travel in what Mr. Von Mierers called the Universal School. At this point they could travel and incarnate in many different worlds and planes in service to our Creator. They served as master souls and free cosmic beings. According to Mierers, there were countless souls who had graduated from numerous different paths, including those on Earth, and had become free to participate in universal projects. In these projects as master souls, they could assist in the spiritual transformation of planets, solar systems, or even entire universes. This explanation resonated with the Ashtar Command's communications from Tuella which explained that volunteer master souls were serving the cause of Light, or higher consciousness, against the darker unconscious energies existing throughout the universe. Master souls from far-flung corners of the universe represented the energies of diverse groups and cultures, they said. Never before had so many of the spiritual hierarchy reincarnated on planet Earth at the same time. Their purpose was clear; to support an awakening humanity's return to "full consciousness," taking its place in the universal family.

As I mentioned earlier, when I asked the Family of Light about the Ashtar Command I was told that the book *Ashtar* would support me in staying connected to them. I found this book incredibly enlightening as it also made me aware of the existence of a celestial governing body, which oversaw the affairs of our universe. It was exciting and comforting for me to contemplate that humanity was part of a greater family of cosmic beings and that the knowledge of a universal governing system was now accessible to all who required it. The Ashtar Command was letting humanity know that this celestial government stands ready to assist in overcoming the many problems we have created and now face on Earth.

They are here to support the souls on planet Earth who are ready and willing to make a shift of awareness and release their many misconceptions regarding UFOs. In a spirit of peace and love, the Ashtar Command will openly work with humanity, both at the personal and governmental level.

In the book *Ashtar*, a group called the Luminarians channels a message from the Ashtar Command that explains the "universal governing system" and its plan to bring humanity into the awareness of the intergalactic life.

The Ashtar Command states that we are all part of the great "multiverse," or cosmos of creation. This is an alliance in which no one group is permitted to direct the affairs of another; only assistance is offered. The Interplanetary Confederation, which is under the command of Ashtar, is the governing body responsible for planet Earth, and operates within our star system only. The Ashtar Command is also linked to the Galactic Confederation, which employs many fleets from a larger group, the Interdimensional Federation of Free Worlds. Through the Luminarians, the Ashtar Command explains that there is a spiritual hierarchy among planets and a hierarchy for the entire solar system. All are tied inexplicably with the Master Jesus, whom they refer to as Jesus Sananda. The Galactic Confederation is no more than four parts of the Interdimensional Federation of Free Worlds. This means the Galactic Confederation of the Milky Way Galaxy. The Galactic Confederation willingly offers support to the Ashtar Command, and whenever additional resources are needed, these can be supplied through the vast resources of the Interdimensional Federation. The Ashtar Command says that such support is being given all the time, and that a being operating at one level of this hierarchy may not be familiar with another level, and may not even have heard the names of other levels. What is being described is millions of personnel and craft from far-flung distant space.

The Interdimensional Federation of Free Worlds is the larger body, being made up of the thirty-three vast sectors of the all-encompassing body. Speaking simply, the Federation is everywhere in the cosmos, which is far greater, far more vast, than anything we can even imagine. To better understand this, the Command gives the following analogy.

"You could think of this solar system as a farm, one of many farms in the state (the galaxy). The farmers' association (the Confederation) is willing to support any individual farmer with whatever he needs to solve his problems. This association cannot, however, issue direct orders to the individual farmer. It's up to the farmer to decide what is best for his own farm. The association can advise or suggest but they cannot enforce. This is the way the galactic governance works. In any vast community of farmers, there is no such thing as a chain of command. On smaller scales, it is possible to have a military structure, but on such a vast scale as the universe, military control is not possible. The only way a chain of command is possible is if the Ashtar Command set it up among themselves, with the support of the Galactic Confederation, as they are only looking after this relatively smaller one-star system."

The Command also explains that while the Galactic Confederation can have a certain amount of standardization, they do not have full standardization from one end to the other. There are simply too many diverse systems, cultures, technologies, and procedures. The Ashtar Command explains that most worlds are not willing to adopt the ways of other worlds even when the other worlds have superior technologies. They admit that although they are unified in spirit, they are far from unified in communication, cultural practices, transportation systems, etc., on either a Confederation or Federation scale.

In the book *Ashtar*, Tuella also shares part of a channeling session she received in El Paso, Texas, from a medium named Gladys Rodehaver. Tuella says that in this session Ashtar himself explains that there are millions of craft operating in this solar system at all times and that many of them belong to the Ashtar Command. Some are stationed far above our planet and are more or less stationary for long periods of time, keeping track of the Earth on their monitoring systems. Others move about, discharging various duties. The small craft might be surveying, for instance, while larger craft with an extended range are capable of operating in space and visiting planets in other solar systems. Ashtar explains that the Ashtar Command has what we would think of as "mother ships" with smaller craft coming and going from them. He says there is a great deal of activity in what human beings think of as empty space. His command and craft are capable of invisibility, and whenever they are traveling beyond the speed of light, they always become invisible to the physical eye. The purpose of the Command, explains Ashtar, is service, and to that end its members will go anywhere they are needed in this sector of space. The headquarters is on one of the largest of the mother crafts; instructions come from this craft, which is a city in itself. Most members of the Command come from one or another of the planets in this solar system, but some are from other solar systems. Ashtar says that some volunteers working with the Command occasionally visit their home planets on what we might call vacations. Most of these souls have worked together in the Command for a very long period of time, and they form an effective and well-knit Confederation.

Coupled with what I had learned through the Ashtar Command material and the Family of Light, there were also countless other books on the array of celestial and angelic support available to humanity. Not only were personal guides, masters, and the Ashtar Command here to support us, we could also request the assistance of angels and the archangels. In her wonderful book called *Messages from Your Angels*, Doreen Virtue describes the archangels' role. She says that part of the archangels' purpose was to oversee guardian angels. Archangels were nondenominational; they would help anyone, regardless of their religious beliefs. The archangels are able to be simultaneously with many different people because they are beyond all restrictions of space and time. Ms. Virtue describes each of them as the patron of a particular sort of person. For instance, Archangel Gabriel is known as the messenger angel and helps all messengers —writers, teachers, journalists, and so on. Archangel Michael is said to release the effects of fear from the planet and its inhabitants, giving humanity the courage to follow our truth and fulfill our divine mission. Michael is also the patron archangel of the upholders of law, such as policemen and women. Archangel Raphael, whose name means "God heals," is in charge of physical healing. He helps all healers, including those people who would like to be healers. We also have Archangel Uriel, whose name means "God is light." He is the one who pours Light upon troubling situations and illuminates our problem-solving abilities. According to Ms. Virtue, we can call upon any of these archangels and servants of God at any time.

On the ascended masters Ms. Virtue describes many of them as beings of Light who have walked our planet as leaders, teachers, and healers, and who now continue to help humanity from their vantage point in the spirit world. These beings have mastered the lessons of earthly life and achieved their ascension, and so they understand what we are going through in our lives because they have, as the saying goes, "been there, done that." Yet, because of the great love they had for the inhabitants of this planet, many have returned to support the evolutionary leap taking place here, as the Family of Light said in one of our sessions.

And so it is. Archangels and master souls from countless dimensions of reality are assisting humanity in a cosmic shift. We were being assured that one way or another, the process of this paradigm shift would bring us all freedom from the dense energies that have enslaved humanity for eons.

Chapter 14
Go forward in the Light

It was now almost twenty years since I first met my dear friend Leslie Kiernan. I remember being so excited to finally meet a healer and medium who could connect me with the spirit realms. Leslie was a true professional at her craft and the most humble of people. My sessions with her continued regularly for over eight years and in that time we became very good friends. Sadly, in 2001, Leslie began to fall ill. She battled the illness bravely and held her sense of humor through her struggle. I would support her as best I could. Sometimes we would just go out for a tea or coffee. One time I drove her to Cape Cod to visit her mother. Even though it was winter time we still took the opportunity to walk along the beach on this extremely blustery day. At one point a sea lion arose from the choppy waters and starred at the both of us as if to say, "What are you doing here on a day like this?" We were freezing but we didn't care. We felt blessed by nature and the sea lion.

Over the following months Leslie would got weaker and her struggle greater. She would be in and out of hospital several times and soon her family and friends realized that her battle was coming to an end. At one point I and some mutual friends sat around her bed and sang My Sweet Lord, which was one of her favorite Beatles songs. The next day, July 17th, Leslie would pass away peacefully back into spirit. I will forever be grateful to her for her spiritual guidance and friendship in my life and also introducing me to the Family of Light whereby I gained the courage and confidence to move forward in sharing the message of the Ashtar Command with many people, including the politicians in Northern Ireland and beyond.

It was almost twenty years since I sent the Ashtar Command material to Gerry Adams and the Irish and British political authorities. The political and social transformation in Ireland following the Republican and Loyalist ceasefires of 1994 was evidence for the entire world to see that when Irelands' leaders worked together they could achieve great things. I believe now that if this same courageous approach from our current leaders towards an Ashtar Command/ UFO disclosure process was to occur, then Ireland could become the gateway to disclosure. If humanity were to invite our celestial family into the halls of government and science, with all their knowledge and advanced technology and offers of support to help us clean up our planet, the world as we know it would be transformed beyond our wildest dreams.

A big step in that direction came in April 2013. An unprecedented event in Washington DC entitled the Citizen Hearing on Disclosure took place, where many researchers, activists, former political leaders and military/agency witnesses representing ten countries gave testimony to six former members of the United States Congress on the evidence for an extraterrestrial presence engaging the human race. When I discovered this event I immediately wished to get involved, so I took the practical step of offering to volunteer at the event. I emailed the Paradigm Research Group (PRG) who were organizing the hearing and simply offered a helping hand in any way I could. To my surprise the head organizer of the event, Steven Bassett, replied offering me a role as a volunteer staff member.

I arrived in Washington on the eve of the hearing, which was scheduled for April 28th through May 1st, 2013. A pre-hearing dinner was also scheduled in the Washington Plaza Hotel where many of the witnesses and several former congressional representatives were staying. I attended the dinner and had a great opportunity to meet my fellow volunteers and some of the witnesses. I was very impressed with Steven Bassett as he welcomed the attendees. He set the tone for what was to become an extremely enlightening week at the National Press Club.

On the opening morning I was filled with anticipation as volunteer staff met and received their assignments before the proceedings began. I was very fortunate that one of my assignments was inside the hearing room. The room was arranged to resemble a Senate hearing room with witness tables, committee tables, press areas, and audience seating. The protocols for congressional hearings were followed as much as possible; the committee members received written statements from witnesses, heard oral statements, and asked whatever questions they wished about the subject matter at hand. The goal of the Citizen Hearing on Disclosure was clear: to bring about Disclosure in 2013 by ending the government truth embargo that prevented the appropriate institutional engagement of the evidence indicating an extraterrestrial presence.

Throughout the hearing I had a sense that even if this unprecedented event did not have an immediate impact in the world, it would certainly play a significant role in eventual disclosure. It was a great testimony to the many brave witnesses that stepped forward to speak their truth.

Just a few weeks after the event the former congressional leaders committee issued a joint communiqué that was displayed on the Citizen Hearing Foundation website. In the communique the leaders pledged their support for the disclosure initiate and requested the Citizen Hearing Foundation use its offices to organize interested parties in a global campaign calling for United Nations sponsorship of a world conference addressing the possible evidence for an extraterrestrial presence engaging this planet.

As a way of continuing to support the disclosure initiative, I intended to promote awareness of this event and the former congressional leader's communiqué in my homeland. This of course was in addition to me publishing my book, with its guidance, wisdom, and knowledge from the Family of Light. However, my plan of action became somewhat delayed; shortly after the disclosure event I began to develop a physical ailment. My good friend recommended that I go see a doctor "just to be on the safe side." After a short consultation with my doctor she advised that I go for a medical test. Within a matter of weeks I had the test, and just a few days later I received a phone call from the medical specialist. The result: cancer. This was not the result I was expecting. To be honest, I don't know what I was expecting, but it wasn't cancer. I was in utter shock.

After breaking this news to my loved ones it became apparent that my only logical move was to return to Ireland, where, along with my family's support, I believed I would beat this disease. I had to; my purpose in this world was not yet complete. I cried out for divine help, as I knew in the depths of my heart that God would see me through this major challenge.

Over the following six months I received so much support through well-wishers, prayers, healing groups, and a wonderful medical team of doctors, surgeons, and nurses. Then, on January 16th 2014, just one week after my operation, my surgeon came to my ward to speak with me. It was the news I had been praying for. I stood by my bed attempting to stand upright as he looked at me and smiled. "Paul. You have had a complete response."

I didn't know what a "complete response" was, but judging by his smile I knew it was good. He explained that the pathologist's report of a complete response meant that there was absolutely no trace of any cancer left in my body. He also said that this result, an "all clear" one week after surgery, was very rare. I felt immense gratitude to him and his team of specialists, and thanked God for granting my wish to "stick around."

And so, I began the process of healing and recovery. I was told it would take six months to a year before I would get back to normal. I took the time to process this major shift in my life; the cancer, resettling in Ireland, where I was with my book project. In the summer of 2014 I decided to enroll in a tour guide course at Belfast Metropolitan College. I believed this would help with my recovery and bring the fun back into my life. After graduating in June 2015 I was ready to return to my book project. In my meditations I was receiving a big nudge from spirit to complete a revision of my book and "get the message out there." I was feeling the strength, courage, and determination to fulfill my promise to God, and I was determined to see this project through. It's my firm belief that, in the not-too-distant future, humanity will openly accept that we are not alone in the universe. Given my own experience with the Family of Light, I have no doubt that humanity will soon welcome benevolent celestial beings from other realms. The process of an awakening humanity continues to increase and will eventually, as the Family of Light has declared, reach a critical mass, and the paradigm shift into the new consciousness will occur.

The Family of Light would often end our sessions with the words "go forward in the light," which I found to be a great source of encouragement. Their words now, more than ever, fill me with a sense determination to share my truth with whoever is inclined to listen. I have felt blessed to have received much direction and guidance in this process. Even though much that the Family of Light had shared with me was specific to my own journey and transformation, most of their guidance was general and applied to anyone seeking a higher reality in life.

In closing, I would like to share these words from the Family of Light, expressing the breadth of the guidance and support they offer to all who seek their love and support:

"It is healing to tune into the Family of Light as you do, for the connection itself brings you a sense of release and relief. We are here for you to connect with until the day comes when your connection with us is part of your constant awareness. For now, stay on your journey, stay on the path, tune in, and be aware of us whenever it pleases you to, for we are here to help you open to receive grace. We will take care of you as best we can. You see, it is a matter of your opening, a matter of your allowing love and grace to enter you. When you forget, we will remind you.

We influence the events of your life, as do you, and all of this effort meshes with and flows into what you call destiny. There is interplay between all of these factors. All of the great ones — the great Light Beings and teachers — who have led the way will continue to support you, uplift you, teach you, and love you.

In the universe there is one love, one Light shining, radiant and beautiful. So, continue to remember that, to pray, to ask for all the help you need, and to stay as open as you can to this assistance.

You have our blessing, now and evermore."

To all my fellow brothers and sisters who have embarked on this amazing journey of the spirit, on planet Earth and in the great beyond, I wish you Godspeed!

Epilogue

When my dear friend Leslie passed away I would still keep in touch with her good friend, named Bonnie. Like Leslie, Bonnie was a healer. She also offered spiritual guidance and had her own spiritual guides speak from the spiritual realms. About five years after Leslie passed I remembered something she said to me in the hospital during one of my final visits. She said, "Paul, don't forget to channel me when I'm gone."

"You're not going anywhere, Leslie," I replied, even though in my heart I knew it was probably our last conversation together, which sadly it was. I decided to share this memory with Bonnie one day. I still had not developed the art of channeling in Leslie and Bonnie's style so I asked if it was possible for her to lead a session and see if Leslie wanted to come through from spirit. Bonnie said, "Yes! Absolutely!"

As we prepared for the session, Bonnie gave thanks for the presence of those spirit guides, angels, beings of Light, and ancestors who were with us. A spirit guide then spoke and told me that of the nine spirits present, one was Leslie Jyoti. Leslie's spiritual name was Jyoti or "Light." The spirit guide then referred to my book. The guide said:

"You are a child of the stars. You are one of us. This is a joyful process. Your life is changing. The writing of this book is the penultimate act of healing. There is so much Light and joy present. Leslie Jyoti is full of joy. She's guiding you. She sends you very much love. She is reminding you to play your music by opening up to the divine melodies within, the melodies that come through your being. This will greatly assist in writing as well. It is the nonlinear, the right-brain functions, through which all creativity is channeled. What you create is then organized and put into coherent form by using the left brain. So both sides of the brain must be exercised if you are to be the most effective and clear channel possible. It is the subconscious mind through which all this information is being channeled, through which it is pouring, and it is the cognitive function that edits and organizes this infinite flow of energy that comes in the form of words."

This spirit guide spoke about how Leslie had been a "way-shower" for me, teaching me how to be a way-shower for others. The guide said that this very book would be a means through which people learned, that by sharing my own spiritual path, I would be reminding people of theirs. Leslie did not speak directly to me through this session but I felt that she was part of a unified message from the various guides and light beings present. The speaker then he said something about me that I feel must be true for many people:

"You had an experience as a child when you were imbued by your guides with a deep consciousness of Light. It is this Light that you have tuned into over and over, through some difficult and very challenging and traumatic circumstances. Because you were imbued

with this consciousness of Light, the Light is always present for you. You received a deep initiation as a child, whether you remember it or not, that has kept you going through some very challenging and dark times. Just as the ancient archetypal yin-yang *symbol demonstrates, in the dark world there is an orb of Light, and in the Light world there is an orb of dark. So dark and Light are connected. On the darkest journey; in the moments of the greatest despair; through struggle, grief, sorrow, and pain, there is always an opening from human consciousness to the Light. It is this journey through the darkness toward the Light that enables souls to mature, to develop deep compassion and a conscious connection to all other beings. This is your role, to be the compassionate way-shower for others, just as Leslie Jyoti was the compassionate way-shower for you.*

You are carrying the torch of truth forward. Keep opening your heart. There are many ways to express this heart-centered truth: through the words that you are transmitting and channeling, through remembering the messages that you have recorded that have become a part of your being; and also through music. Music will become even more significant in your life.

Your simplicity and humility have served you well. Remember that you are a child of the stars. Sometimes, in the course of this lifetime and prior lifetimes, you have felt cosmic loneliness, alienation, despair; you have felt separate and apart. You have come to this point through several incarnations to learn that you are never apart, never separate from Source, from love itself. You are never alone. You are continually watched over."

This compassionate and enlightening session through Bonnie's guides seems to me to be the essence of what I received from the Family of Light throughout my cosmic quest: a message of hope, a message of union, a message of universal love. Since the completion of this book is "the penultimate act of healing" for me, I listened carefully to see if I would learn what the ultimate, or final, act of healing might be. That was not described, but I trust that I will learn about it when the time is right.

At the end of this session, I thanked the beings who had come to share their wisdom, knowing that I made this offering of gratitude not just for myself, but for each and every one of the souls who might benefit in the future from this book.

Bibliography

Essene, Virginia. *New Teachings for an Awakening Humanity.* Out-of-Print from Publisher S.E.E Publishing Co, Santa Clara, California, USA. Possibly available from on-line used book sources.

Montgomery, Ruth. *Companions Along the Way,* (Coward, McCann & Geoghegan, 1970.

Tuella. *Ashtar.* Inner Light Publications. 1994.

Zukav, Gary. *Seat of the Soul* 25th *anniversary edition.* Simon and Schuster. 2014.

Recommended Websites

Inward Journey, Diandra, www.inwardjourney.com

Share Foundation, www.sharefoundationnetwork.com

Paradigm Research Group, www.paradigmresearchgroup.org

Planetary Activation Organization, Sheldan Nidle, www.paoweb.com

Dr. Kathryn E. May www.whoneedslight.org

About the Author

Paul Gavan was born in 1966 in Belfast, Northern Ireland, and as he was growing up, he experienced at first-hand the devastating effects of the conflict in what was Europe's longest war. In his early twenties, Paul began to question his life, undergoing a transformation that led him to leave Ireland in search of spiritual enlightenment. This book is a record of that journey to date, including the communications — the teachings, observations, advice, and predictions — that Paul has received from his spirit guides and the Family of Light. Working through a spiritual medium, Paul posed questions to spirits that communicated from higher-dimensional realms to offer him guidance.

Paul is sharing this guidance now because, as the Family of Light told him, it applies not only to him but to all of humanity. It is Paul's wish that by publishing this book, it will support the expansion of consciousness that is taking place on Earth as humanity enters a new era of collective enlightenment. Paul is currently living in Belfast, N. Ireland. He would be happy to reply to any questions regarding his book and can be reached at:

paulgavan7@yahoo.com and on Facebook at www.facebook.com/My-Cosmic-Quest

Leslie Kiernan 4th May 1954 – 17th July 2002

Printed in the United States
by Baker & Taylor Publisher Services

Printed in the United States
by Baker & Taylor Publisher Services